D0758498

CALGARY PUBLIC LIBRARY

MAY ⁄ ⁄ 2004

Exploring **C**anada

SASKATCHEWAN

Titles in the Exploring Canada series include:

Alberta

British Columbia

Manitoba

Ontario

Quebec

Yukon Territory

Exploring Canada

SASKATCHEWAN

by Mark Mayell

LUCENT
BOOKS®

THOMSON
™
GALE

San Diego • Detroit • New York • San Francisco • Cleveland • New Haven, Conn. • Waterville, Maine • London • Munich

Development, management, design, and composition by Pre-Press Company, Inc.

© 2003 by Lucent Books. Lucent Books is an imprint of The Gale Group, Inc.,
a division of Thomson Learning, Inc.

Lucent Books® and Thomson Learning™ are trademarks used herein under license.

For more information, contact
Lucent Books
27500 Drake Rd.
Farmington Hills, MI 48331-3535
Or you can visit our Internet site at http://www.gale.com

ALL RIGHTS RESERVED.
No part of this work covered by the copyright hereon may be reproduced or used in any form or by
any means—graphic, electronic, or mechanical, including photocopying, recording, taping, Web distribution or information storage retrieval systems—without the written permission of the publisher.

LIBRARY OF CONGRESS CATALOGING-IN-PUBLICATION DATA

Mayell, Mark,
Saskatchewan. / by Mark Mayell.
    v. cm. — (Exploring Canada series)
Includes bibliographical references and index.
Contents: Saskatchewan.—Prairies, parklands, mountains, and
forests—The fur trade and the Land of Living Skies—Settling the West—Life in
Saskatchewan today—Arts and culture—Facing the future—Facts about Saskatchewan.
  ISBN 1-59018-052-6 (hardback : alk. paper)
  1. Saskatchewan.—Juvenile literature. 2. Saskatchewan.—History—Juvenile
literature. [1. Saskatchewan. 2. Canada.] I. Mayell, Mark II. Title. III.
Series.
F1062.4 .M39 2003
  971.27—dc21   2002003815

Printed in the United States of America

Contents

Foreword

Any truly accurate portrait of Canada would have to be painted in sharp contrasts, for this is a long-inhabited but only recently settled land. It is a vast and expansive region peopled by a predominantly urban population. Canada is also a nation of natives and immigrants that, as its Prime Minister Lester Pearson remarked in the late 1960s, has "not yet found a Canadian soul except in time of war." Perhaps it is in these very contrasts that this elusive national identity is waiting to be found.

Canada as an inhabited place is among the oldest in the Western Hemisphere, having accepted prehistoric migrants more than eleven thousand years ago after they crossed a land bridge where the Bering Strait now separates Alaska from Siberia. Canada is also the site of the New World's earliest European settlement, L'Anse aux Meadows on the northern tip of Newfoundland Island. A band of Vikings lived there briefly some five hundred years before Columbus reached the West Indies in 1492.

Yet as a nation Canada is still a relative youngster on the world scene. It gained its independence almost a century after the American Revolution and half a century after the wave of nationalist uprisings in South America. Canada did not include Newfoundland until 1949 and could not amend its own constitution without approval from the British Parliament until 1982. "The Sleeping Giant," as Canada is sometimes known, came within a whisker of losing a province in 1995, when the people of Quebec narrowly voted down an independence referendum. In 1999 Canada carved out a new territory, Nunavut, which has a population equal to that of Key West, Florida, spread over an area the size of Alaska and California combined.

As the second largest country in the world (after Russia), the land itself is also famously diverse. British Columbia's "Pocket Desert" near the town of Osoyoos is the northernmost desert in North America. A few hundred miles away, in Alberta's Banff National Park, one can walk on the Columbia Icefields, the largest nonpolar icecap in the world. In parts of Manitoba and the Yukon glacially created sand dunes creep slowly across the landscape. Quebec and Ontario have so many lakes in the boundless north that tens of thousands remain unnamed.

One can only marvel at a place where the contrasts range from the profound (the first medical use of insulin) to the mundane (the invention of Trivial Pursuit); the sublime (the poetry of Ontario-born Robertson Davies) to the ridiculous (the comic antics of Ontario-born Jim Carrey); the British (ever-so-quaint Victoria) to the French (Montreal, the world's second-largest French-speaking city); and the environmental (Greenpeace was founded in Vancouver) to the industrial (refuse from nickel mining near Sudbury, Ontario, left a landscape so barren that American astronauts used it to train for their moon walks).

Given these contrasts and conflicts, can this national experiment known as Canada survive? Or to put it another way, what is it that unites as Canadians the elderly Inuit woman selling native crafts in the Yukon; the millionaire businessman-turned-restaurateur recently emigrated from Hong Kong to Vancouver; the mixed-French (Métis) teenager living in a rural settlement in Manitoba; the cosmopolitan French-speaking professor of archaeology in Quebec City; and the raw-boned Nova Scotia fisherman struggling to make a living? These are questions only Canadians can answer, and perhaps will have to face for many decades.

A true portrait of Canada cannot, therefore, be provided by a brief essay, any more than a snapshot captures the entire life of a centenarian. But the Exploring Canada series can offer an illuminating overview of individual provinces and territories. Each book smartly summarizes an area's geography, history, arts and culture, daily life, and contemporary issues. Read individually or as a series, they show that what Canadians undeniably have in common is a shared heritage as people who came, whether in past millennia or last year, to a land with a difficult climate and a challenging geography, yet somehow survived and worked with one another to form a vibrant whole.

The Heartland of Canada

Located close to the geographical center of North America, Saskatchewan is sometimes called the heartland of Canada. The province is internationally famous for its expansive farms and stately wooden grain elevators. While Saskatchewan may be "the wheatbasket province" and "middle Canada," beneath the white-bread surface identity lurks a province that can be surprisingly progressive in its politics, diverse in its culture, and varied in its landscape.

The region has long been identified with cooperative political movements, like those that rural grain farmers organized even before the establishment of the province in 1905. Provincial politicians have passed progressive laws relating to trade unions, minimum wages, and workers' holidays. And it was Saskatchewan that elected the first socialist government (one that advocates collective ownership of key industries) in North America and pioneered the government-funded health care system now embraced throughout Canada. Saskatchewan's reputation for political activism and social justice has continued in recent years. *Maclean's* columnist Alan Fotheringham called its premier for most of the 1990s, Roy Romanow, "the Ukrainian Redford"[1]—alluding to the actor who is as famous for his causes as he is for his roles. Unlike a number of other provinces, Saskatchewan has not privatized the public corporations that provide residents with electricity and telephone service. Even the official provincial motto, "From many peoples, strength," points to an emphasis on community and cooperation that contrasts with, for example, neighboring Alberta's "strong and free."

Culturally, Saskatchewan may be less openly hip than west coast "Bee Cee" (British Columbia) but it has a higher

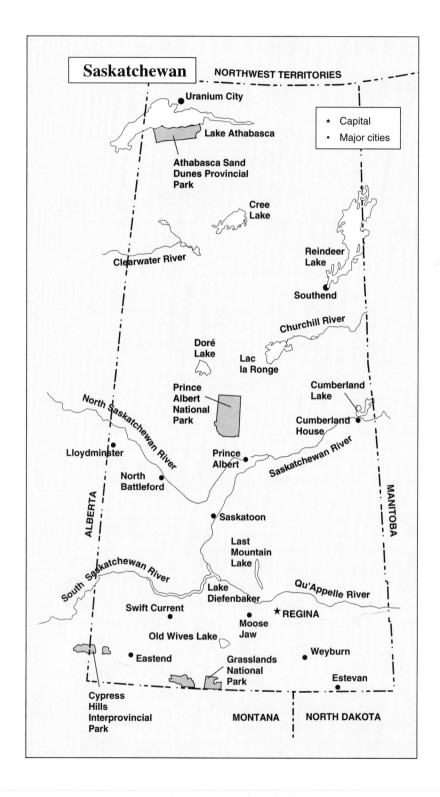

Saskatchewan

NORTHWEST TERRITORIES

★ Capital
• Major cities

• Uranium City

Lake Athabasca

Athabasca Sand
Dunes Provincial
Park

Cree
Lake

Reindeer
Lake

Clearwater River

• Southend

Churchill River

Doré
Lake

Lac
la Ronge

Prince
Albert
National
Park

Cumberland
Lake

Cumberland •
House

North Saskatchewan River

Lloydminster •

Prince
Albert •

Saskatchewan River

North •
Battleford

ALBERTA

• Saskatoon

Last
Mountain
Lake

MANITOBA

South Saskatchewan River

Lake
Diefenbaker

Qu'Appelle River

Swift Current •

★ REGINA

Moose
Jaw •

Old Wives Lake

• Eastend

Grasslands
National
Park

• Weyburn

Estevan
•

Cypress
Hills
Interprovincial
Park

MONTANA   NORTH DAKOTA

ratio of urban to rural residents (approximately two to one) than that of the maritime provinces and an increasingly diverse citizenry. Perhaps not surprising given Saskatchewan's obviously Indian name (it is derived from a Cree term for "swift-flowing river"), the province has a higher percentage of natives than all but the Northwest Territories and Nunavut. Saskatchewan was a pioneer in public support for the arts and today harbors a thriving film and video industry, supports annual jazz and fringe performing arts festivals, and is home to renowned painters.

Contrary to its reputation as a land of wheat fields and little else, Saskatchewan encompasses beneath its spectacularly broad skies sprawling landscapes of remarkable beauty and diversity. It is true that, like Alberta, Saskatchewan is landlocked. Yet Saskatchewan has two of Canada's largest lakes mostly within its borders, and the double-branched Saskatchewan River is one of the country's major arteries. It is also true that, like Manitoba, its neighbor to the east, Saskatchewan is widely viewed as a strictly prairie province. Yet more than half of Saskatchewan's area, including all of the sparsely populated north, is not prairie but forest and uplands.

Even the prairie landscape that does dominate southern Saskatchewan is hardly a uniform sheet of wheat, although there are wide expanses of farmland. Especially along the province's border with Montana and North Dakota the prairies are interrupted by dramatic badlands, where Tyrannosaurus rex and other dinosaurs stalked the area when it was

■ *Saskatchewan's flag has a western red lily and the provincial shield of arms, with its red lion (a traditional royal symbol) and three gold wheat sheaves.*

■ *Saskatoon's evening lights shimmer on the South Saskatchewan River.*

the edge of a vast inland sea. In the Cypress Hills in the southwest, an unnamed elevation of 4,567 feet (1,392 meters) is the highest point between the Rockies and the Torngat Mountains on the Quebec/Labrador border. The prairies and an adjoining parkland belt also hold Saskatchewan's half dozen small but bustling cities.

A Uniquely Canadian Place

Although farming remains a major enterprise in Saskatchewan—the province has more than 40 percent of Canada's cultivated land and grows greater quantities of wheat, oats, flaxseed, canola, lentils, mustard seed, and peas than any other province or territory—fewer than one in six provincial residents is employed through agriculture. Spurred on by the economic disaster of the Great Depression of the 1930s (which Saskatchewan residents still refer to as the "Dirty Thirties"), Saskatchewan has increasingly developed a more diversified economy that seeks to exploit mining, forestry, and energy resources, including considerable reserves of oil and coal. Over the past decade the province has also become more aggressive in developing tourism as well as industries based on food products, information technology, software development, and biomedical research. Companies have opened new electronics assembly plants, telephone call and data processing centers, banks, and insurance operations. The University of Saskatchewan in Saskatoon is building one of the world's few synchrotons, a $200 million, football-field-sized "super microscope" for advanced particle research.

Despite impressive efforts at diversifying the provincial economy, Saskatchewan today faces difficult social and political challenges. Its economy remains somewhat dependent upon world prices set for both agricultural commodities and fuels. When world supply exceeds demand and prices fall—as they did for wheat and oil during a number of recent years—Saskatchewan's economy sputters rather than purrs. Many rural towns that have tried to rely solely on farming for their economic foundation are losing population and shutting schools. As residents leave farms, small towns, and Indian reserves (reservations)for the two main cities of Regina (pronounced rih-JY-nuh) and Saskatoon, urban schools become crowded and city streets see rising crime rates. The tough times have even caused significant numbers of Saskatchewan's best and brightest to leave for Alberta, Ontario, and the United States for better jobs and wages.

Those who remain in Saskatchewan are a determined breed, willing to endure periods of struggle while maintaining a faith in the power of collective action. In the mid-1960s the Canadian radio icon Peter Gzowski noted that many of the people of Saskatchewan "seem to be close to the land in a way that no other non-French Canadians are." Gzowski wrote:

> A thing I want to say about the Canadian heartland is how completely Canadian it is, at least in the sense that it is not American. Nearly every other important population centre in Canada is twinned by geography to a large American city: Vancouver-Seattle, Toronto-Buffalo, etc. Calgary and Edmonton have imported enough Americans not to have to go anywhere to hear someone ask for cawfee. But if you drive due south from Regina the distance between Saint John, N.B., and Boston, you end up on the outskirts of Ismay, Montana. Consequently you do not drive due south. . . . A by-product of this isolation is that . . . when a trend like the anti-eggheadism of the early 1950s sweeps the United States—even though, as that particular one did, it seems to have its motherlode in the American Midwest—Saskatchewan can remain untouched, and Canadian.[2]

To a certain extent this portrait of a remote and isolated Saskatchewan has been overtaken by advances in communications and transportation technology. Satellite dishes receive American television programs, and Saskatchewan's young are hardly immune to the latest American-inspired trends in music and fashion. Yet it is true that Saskatchewan remains a distinctly Canadian place, proud of its political and cultural heritage and intent on preserving its uniqueness.

Land of Living Skies

S askatchewan may not deserve its reputation for squareness in a cultural sense but geographically it does: It is the only Canadian province or territory with exclusively artificial, straight-line borders. The 49th parallel of latitude forms the southern edge of the province, as it does for all of Canada from Manitoba to British Columbia's Strait of Georgia, and the 60th parallel of latitude separates Saskatchewan from the Northwest Territories. The 110th line of longitude marks the western border with Alberta. On the east the 102nd longitude line is the border with Manitoba in the north. South of Saskatchewan's Reindeer Lake, however, the eastern border zigzags off the line to accommodate the square town lines surveyors imposed on the Great Plains before the province was created in 1905.

These borders make Saskatchewan roughly rectangular in shape. It is approximately 400 miles (640 kilometers) wide at its broadest along the U.S. border, 275 miles (440 kilometers) across at its northernmost point, and 750 miles (1,200 kilometers) from south to north. It is the fifth-largest Canadian province, slightly larger than Manitoba and a little smaller than the state of Texas. It is this broad geographic reach, in combination with the province's midcontinent location and its unique geologic history, that have helped to create such a diversity of landforms, wildlife, and natural resources.

An Ancient Geologic Legacy

The landscape of the province owes a number of its features to geologic forces and events that occurred millions and even

Canada's Capitals and Major Cities

billions of years ago. The bedrock known as the Canadian or the Precambrian Shield underlies much of Saskatchewan. It is among the oldest geologic formations on the earth's surface—rocks found in Saskatchewan have been dated to more than 2.5 billion years. In the northern half of the province, where layers of this ancient bedrock lack a sedimentary cover and thus lie exposed, the rolling hills and poorly drained soil make for a landscape of shallow lakes and meandering rivers.

Until approximately 65 million years ago, much of the southern half of the province was covered by an inland sea that extended over the eastern half of North America. The area's climate was much warmer and more humid than it is today and the dinosaurs that roamed the surrounding forests and swamplands fed on ancient fern- and palmlike plants, giant oaks and magnolias, and aquatic grasses. Remnants of this ancient landscape include the rich deposits of oil and natural gas that have been discovered in Saskatchewan.

More recently (by geologic standards), massive ice sheets covered all of the province except for its highest areas, particularly around the Cypress Hills. Continental glaciers formed and melted at least five times, from about 2 million years ago until as recently as twelve thousand years ago, when the last one began its retreat to the polar ice cap of today. These glaciers scrubbed Saskatchewan's surface and left behind rocky moraines and other notable landscape features. When the glaciers melted during warm periods, huge lakes formed. It is the deposited sediments left behind from the bottom of these now-evaporated lakes that account for the dark, rich soil of the prairie and the fertility of the province's wheat and grain farms.

Saskatchewan's territory today ranges from the mixed grasslands of the south to the almost treeless uplands in the Canadian Shield of the far north. Much local variation and some unique ecological zones can be found, however, in the transitions from prairie to parkland to forest.

Prairie Grasslands

The prairie that most people consider Saskatchewan's dominant landscape is limited to the southern third of the province, extending somewhat farther north on the western border to the area of Lloydminster. Saskatchewan's prairie is the northernmost extension of the Great Plains of central North America, the relatively flat, arid, and treeless grasslands that once supported immense herds of bison (buffalo). The original mixed-grass prairie that existed in present-day Saskatchewan two centuries ago, before the advent of grain farming and cattle ranching, now can be found mainly in patches in Grasslands National Park just north of the Montana border and in a few other places. The province's prairie environment includes a few large lakes, such as Old Wives and human-made Lake Diefenbaker, but none compare with the innumerable, and sometimes enormous, lakes of the north. Some of the prairie's more shallow lakes and smaller creeks have a habit of disappearing entirely by the end of a dry summer.

Native prairie grasslands are capable of supporting a variety of animals, birds, and insects. Some of the animals that were once found in huge numbers in the prairies of Saskatchewan, such as buffalo, greater prairie chickens (a type of grouse), burrowing owls, and prairie dogs, are now gone or exist only in limited numbers. For example, Saskatchewan's

■ Prairie Dogs: A Keystone Species

Saskatchewan's few remaining prairie dogs are of the black-tailed variety, the most common of the five North American species. These small, social rodents are typically about a foot long and two pounds in weight. They have pale brown coats, a white underbody, sharp claws, and black-tipped tails. They use their claws to dig burrows that may go fifteen feet (five meters) deep and branch out at different levels for separate sleeping and eating chambers. Colonies are subdivided into "wards" and even smaller "coteries," one coterie to a burrow. A coterie typically includes a male, one to four females, and offspring less than two years old. Coterie members have been observed grooming, hugging, and "kissing" (touching incisors, a recognition tactic). The burrows have limited connections but residents of any ward have plenty of interaction and opportunity to employ their surprisingly elaborate system of communication.

Prairie dogs speak to each other by using postures as well as a dozen or so distinct calls, from yips to barks. A major function of their communication is to warn of the approach of such predators as coyotes, weasels, and badgers. Notably absent from this list of predators is the prairie dog's second most-deadly enemy (after humans), the black-footed ferret. Its numbers have been so reduced that researchers thought the species extinct until a small population was discovered in Wyoming in 1981.

once extensive prairie dog colonies now number perhaps two dozen, mostly scattered throughout the rangelands of the Frenchman River valley and nearby Grasslands National Park. These colonies are the only ones left in Canada. (Prairie dogs have managed to survive in greater numbers in the United States.)

A number of animals have survived humanity's taming of the prairies somewhat better than the buffalo and prairie dog. For example, the southern prairie's ponds often harbor high numbers of ducks and geese. Other grassland birds and animals include western meadowlarks, coyote, mule deer, horned lizards, and western painted turtles.

Badlands, Hills, and Sand Dunes

The gently rolling southern prairies take on a more showy appearance in a number of places, with the landscape ranging from rugged badlands to sand dunes. Not far from where Saskatchewan's southern border meets both Montana and

If provincial names like Prairie Dog Drive-In, *Prairie Dog Magazine,* and Prairie Dog Farm are any indication, Saskatchewan residents have belatedly embraced this embattled animal as a symbol of their plains heritage. Today, both federal and provincial laws recognize prairie dogs as a vulnerable species and grant them protection from being disturbed or killed. Even so, prairie dog numbers have been slow to increase over the past decade. Because prairie dogs are a "keystone species" connected through a complex web of interactions to many other animals, their survival would be good news for creatures that feed on the rodents or use their burrows, including Canada's distinctive but threatened burrowing owl.

■ *A black-tailed prairie dog eats grass in an open field.*

North Dakota, the cliffs, valleys, "hogbacks" (steeply sloped ridges), and grass-covered hills of the Big Muddy Badlands create a stunning visual backdrop to the surrounding plains. A major feature of the badlands is Castle Butte, an isolated, wedding-cake-shaped, 200-foot- (60-meter) high sandstone outcropping that is pocked with caves. From the flat summit, hikers are afforded an inspiring view of a stark valley carved by glacial meltwater. The valley is almost 2 miles (3 kilometers) wide and up to 500 feet (160 meters) deep.

Sitting Bull's Sioux warriors sought refuge within the Big Muddy after wiping out Custer's Seventh Cavalry troops at the Battle of the Little Big Horn in Montana in 1876, and other native tribes once walked among the prickly pear cactus and sagebrush of these badlands. Today the badlands are mainly home to wildlife like mule deer, antelope, golden eagles, red-tailed hawks, and even a few rattlesnakes. Although much of the area is privately owned ranch land, there are places where people are welcome to explore, and guided tours are also available.

■ *Much of the Big Muddy Badlands in southern Saskatchewan is a rugged landscape of eroded sandstone.*

Another interesting break in the prairies of southern Saskatchewan occurs farther west, near the border with Alberta. For those approaching from the east, the Cypress Hills highlands that erupt from the plains appear "a perfect oasis in the desert,"[3] as nineteenth-century surveyor John Palliser noted. Most of the upland plateau is sixteen hundred feet (five hundred meters) or more above the plains. The area includes rolling grasslands, forested hills of white spruce and trembling aspen, and numerous streams and ponds.

The highest elevations harbor animal and plant species that are unusual for southern Saskatchewan, including snowshoe hare and stands of lodgepole pine reminiscent of the Rockies. (There are no true cypress trees—the area's name is actually a misnomer from the early voyageurs, the canoe-borne French fur traders, who called the lodgepole pines *cyprès,* their name for the jack pines of Quebec. When Palliser's surveying party came through the area in the late 1850s and marked it as the Cypress Hills on their maps, the name stuck.) Hikers and campers may also spot pronghorn antelope, coyote, and white-tailed deer. The area is a favorite among birders for its yellow-rumped warblers, mountain bluebirds, wild turkeys, and trumpeter swans. Some of the most scenic uplands have been preserved in Cypress Hills Interprovincial Park, part of which Saskatchewan shares with Alberta.

North of the U.S.-Canadian border, where the open grasslands get somewhat more rain, is prime wheat growing territory as well as the province's major metropolitan areas of Regina and Saskatoon. The broad grain fields are interrupted by occasional river valleys like the Qu'Appelle, with its stands of aspens and populations of red fox, jack rabbits, and white-tailed deer. (The river's French name is from a melancholy Cree legend about a young man who replied "Qu'appelle?"— "Who calls?"—when he heard someone call his name as he crossed a valley lake. He heard only his echo in response, but later determined his name was being called by his bride-to-be at the instant of her death.)

A Parkland Belt

Between the grasslands of the south and the forests of the north, Saskatchewan has a parkland belt that includes some of the most charming landscapes in the province. The parkland belt is broadest in the southeastern corner of Saskatchewan and narrows as it angles across the province, roughly between Saskatoon and the central city of Prince Albert.

■ A Rare Sand Dune Area

The desertlike Great Sand Hills in southwestern Saskatchewan, below the South Saskatchewan River, are a spectacular sight. Sand dunes are fifty feet (fifteen meters) high and three hundred feet (one hundred meters) long. Those that are bare of plant life may be moved by the prevailing westerly winds up to fifteen feet (five meters) per year. Other dunes have been stabilized by cactus, saskatoon (serviceberry) and other shrubs, native grasses, and cottonwood trees. Children love to explore the rolling landscape and jump from sandy precipices.

The 750-square-mile (1,900-square-kilometer) Great Sand Hills area is not a provincial park although the province owns much of the land. Because energy companies recently discovered that the hills contain oil and natural gas deposits, disputes have arisen between developers, private property owners, and environmentalists. In the 1990s four small towns in the Great Sand Hills formed a joint commission and agreed to a plan that designates certain parts of the area for ranching, oil and gas development, and preservation. The provincial government also includes some of the Great Sand Hills in a protected areas program.

■ *A female moose and her calf forage in one of Saskatchewan's national parks.*

Much of the land is cultivated in wheat, canola, and barley but there are also spruce bogs, groves of aspen, and glacially carved lakes. In the more northern parts of the belt are hilly uplands and the beginning of the rolling evergreen forests of white spruce and jack pine that dominate the north. Some of the province's most heavily logged forests are within the parkland belt, as are a number of popular provincial parks including Greenwater Lake, Moose Mountain, and The Battlefords.

The mixed habitat of the parkland belt provides shelter for animals ranging from large mammals (including moose, elk, and black bear) to migratory waterfowl. The animal whose sought-after pelt drove the early history of Canada, the beaver, thrives in many of the lakes and streams of this part of Saskatchewan. Among the many birds that can be spotted are gray jays, boreal chickadees, western kingbirds, and yellow-headed blackbirds.

Located sixty miles (one hundred kilometers) east of Saskatoon is one of the more unusual lakes in this region. Little Manitou Lake is a shallow, finger-shaped, fourteen-mile-(twenty-three-kilometer) long body filled with mineral-laden water. Little Manitou's water, which comes from underground springs, is packed with sodium, magnesium, and potassium. The lake water's specific density is 50 percent greater than that of the Middle East's Dead Sea, and Little Manitou is more than three times saltier than any ocean. People have been known to sit on the dense water while calmly reading the newspaper. Native Americans have long considered the lake waters to have spiritual and healing properties, and they refrained from waging battle near the "Lake of the Good Spirit." Today many people visit the European–spa-like facilities, including the largest indoor mineral pool in Canada, in Manitou Beach.

Forests and Wetlands of the North

The upper half of Saskatchewan—roughly everything north of Prince Albert National Park—is a sparsely populated land of marshes, evergreen forests, and lakes. Within this vast area the environment is diverse enough to include the hilly plains and level plateaus of Narrow Hills Provincial Park, the wetlands of the Cumberland Lake area on the border with Manitoba, and the narrow canyons and limestone cliffs of Clearwater River Provincial Park. Most of Saskatchewan's extensive forests, encompassing an area the size of Montana, are located within the northern half of the province. Deciduous trees like American elm, aspen, and Manitoba maple are more common around Lac La Ronge Provincial Park than farther north where balsam fir, jack pine, and white spruce predominate. The great coniferous forest, also known as taiga, covers much of northern Saskatchewan as it sweeps across Canada from Newfoundland to British Columbia.

North of Lac La Ronge the province is within the permafrost zone. Soil at various depths stays frozen year-round, making agriculture impractical and limiting tree size. All of Saskatchewan, however, is within Canada's wooded country. In this respect it differs from Manitoba, whose northeast section, along the Hudson Bay, is treeless tundra. The closest Saskatchewan comes to a subarctic environment is the lake-strewn uplands along the border with the Northwest Territories. This area is characterized by stands of stunted black spruce and jack pine, exposed bedrock, glacial features such as eskers (sinuous ridges) and drumlins (elongated hills), and lichen and other low-growing ground cover. The rugged ridges and hills rise at one point to reach a treeless peak of 1,625 feet (495 meters).

A Region of Giant Lakes

Huge lakes dominate the northern third of Saskatchewan. Lake Athabasca, which Saskatchewan shares with Alberta, and Reindeer Lake, which extends into Manitoba, are the fourth- and fifth-largest lakes in Canada (not including the

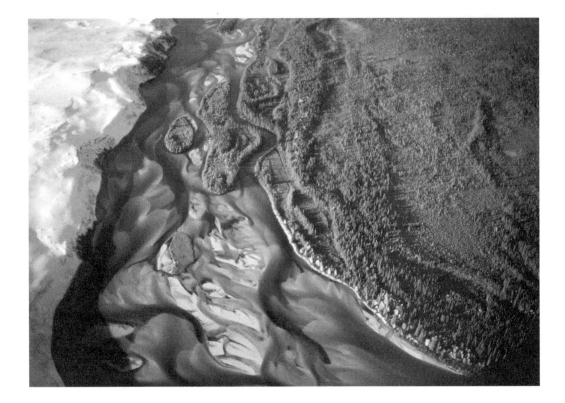

■ *The William River forms a scenic delta of sandbars and shallow channels as it flows through Athabasca Sand Dunes Provincial Park and enters Lake Athabasca.*

Great Lakes that are partly in the United States). Athabasca and Reindeer are mighty not only by Canadian standards but by world standards, being among the twenty-five largest lakes on the planet. Together Athabasca and Reindeer cover more surface area than the state of Connecticut. Wollaston Lake and Cree Lake, west of Reindeer, are smaller but still large enough that, if they were in the United States, they would rank among the country's largest freshwater lakes.

Athabasca features an unusual sand dune region that is similar to the one at the Great Sand Hills some 600 miles (970 kilometers) to the south. The Athabasca Sand Dunes Provincial Park, located on the southern shores of the lake, features the most northerly set of major dune fields in the world and the largest active sand surface in Canada. The Athabasca Sand Dunes stretch for about sixty miles (one hundred kilometers), with individual dunes soaring as high as one hundred feet (thirty meters). The park holds dozens of rare plant species, including a few (such as sand chickweed and Mackenzie hairgrass) that are found nowhere else on Earth.

Geologists speculate that meltwater from retreating glaciers began to deposit sand sediments and form the dunes around eight thousand years ago. Today the dunes are still on the move, slowly engulfing the forest in one area and revealing the dead remnants of another forest elsewhere.

At 2,568 square miles (6,651 square kilometers), Reindeer Lake is only slightly smaller than Lake Athabasca and is not quite as remote—one road reaches the southern end in Saskatchewan and another touches the eastern shore at the Manitoba border. Most of the year-round inhabitants are First Nations (native Indian) people. The Southend Indian Reserve at the southernmost tip of the lake is one of the many reserves under the jurisdiction of the Peter Ballantyne Cree Nation.

The extreme depth of Reindeer—more than 700 feet (213 meters) in some places—keeps the water cold even during the summer. This makes Reindeer one of the best places in North America to catch trophy-size arctic grayling as well as northern pike, walleye, and lake trout. A number of lodges located on the shores of Reindeer cater to sport fishing, offering Cree guides, float planes, lodging, and equipment.

Reindeer, about five-sixths of which is located within Saskatchewan, drains a large part of northeast Saskatchewan and northwest Manitoba. The Reindeer River that flows out of the southern end of the lake connects with the Churchill River system that flows east across Manitoba to the Hudson Bay. Lake Athabasca, on the other hand, drains to the northwest. Its waters flow through the Great Slave Lake in the Northwest Territories and eventually reach, via the Mackenzie River, the Arctic's Beaufort Sea. Many of northern Saskatchewan's smaller lakes are poorly drained. The province's one massive river system is located to the south, where it has long played a central role in transportation, agriculture, and wildlife.

A River Highway to the Heartland

The fourth-longest river entirely in Canada, the Saskatchewan River is one of the most important rivers in Canada. The Cree knew it as *Kisiskatchewani Sipi,* or "swift-flowing river," with the English transliteration "Saskatchewan" first officially applied to the region when a new district of the North-West Territories was created in 1882. Natives have fished the river's two main branches, the North and the South, and hunted its valleys for thousands of years. In the decades preceding the completion of Canada's transcontinental railway in the 1880s, two-hundred-foot (sixty-meter) sternwheeler riverboats cruised the Saskatchewan and carried settlers into the prairies. The river's overall influence, however, has hardly declined in the twentieth century. It remains a crucial asset used for generating power, irrigating fields, and providing recreation.

The North and South Saskatchewan both begin in the Rocky Mountains of western Alberta, with the North generally flowing through the parkland belt on the northern edge of the prairies and the South being a true prairie river. The North Saskatchewan originates as a stream tumbling from the Saskatchewan Glacier, part of the Columbia Icefields in Alberta's Banff National Park. An early fur-trading fort on its banks eventually grew into the city of Edmonton. The North Saskatchewan flows east across the Alberta-Saskatchewan line a little north of Lloydminster. The river and its parkland valley continues east before veering north and heading for its junction with the South Saskatchewan about thirty miles (fifty kilometers) east of Prince Albert.

The South Saskatchewan starts from the confluence of several smaller rivers that flow east off the Continental Divide in southwestern Alberta and northwestern Montana, not far from where the northern branch originates. Like the North, the South relies on mountain snowmelt and its Alberta tributaries for much of its volume before entering arid southern Saskatchewan. The river turns north through prairie grasslands about sixty miles (one hundred kilometers) south of Saskatoon, where it has been dammed to form Lake Diefenbaker. The South flows through Saskatoon and is roughly parallel to the North as the two branches approach Prince Albert, where they turn east and merge.

Beyond the confluence of the North and South at "The Forks," the Saskatchewan River flows through Tobin Lake and into the marshy lowland delta west of Cumberland Lake. From there it flows into Manitoba near the lumbering town of The Pas and empties into Cedar Lake, and then through Grand Rapids into Lake Winnipeg. The Saskatchewan River's basin in its entirety encompasses a California-sized chunk of the three prairie provinces and is home to more than 3 million people. Ultimately this water, which originated as a trickle in the Rocky

Mountains, is carried by the Nelson River all the way to the Hudson Bay. Unfortunately for Saskatchewan, the river system in Manitoba flows over a steeper gradient, allowing Manitoba to harness much more hydroelectric power than Saskatchewan does from its three Saskatchewan River hydro stations.

A Continental Climate

Saskatchewan's location and geography are major factors in determining its climate. The province is situated in the northern middle part of the continent. It is therefore far from the Atlantic and Pacific oceans, which are potential sources of precipitation and generally moderating effects on temperature. Saskatchewan is also affected by the Rocky Mountains in western Alberta. Clouds being pushed by the prevailing winds from the west tend to drop their precipitation as they gain altitude to pass over the mountain range, causing the relatively wet weather of British Columbia and the relatively dry weather of the prairie provinces. Saskatchewan's location makes it susceptible to arctic air masses that sweep down from the north. Saskatchewan's mostly flat landscape provides few obstacles for winds. All of these factors combine to make Saskatchewan in general a dry and windy place that experiences dramatic storms and wide variations in seasonal temperatures. Saskatchewan is also one of the sunniest regions in North America.

In the southern part of the province summer days can be very hot. In fact Canada's hottest temperature on record occurred in southeastern Saskatchewan on July 5, 1937, when the thermometer hit 113° F (45° C) in Midale and Yellow Grass. Parts of the southwest enjoy 160 frost-free days per year. The prairies are arid—Regina averages less than two inches (five centimeters) of rain every month except June. Winters are also relatively dry. Although annual snowfall on the prairies is low, the freezing weather allows snow to last for months and it sometimes accumulates in deep drifts. Average daily temperatures in Regina are below 10° F (−12° C) from December through February.

In the far north, average year-round temperatures are much lower. This is not surprising, since the distance between Saskatchewan's southern and northern borders is similar to the distance in latitude between Cleveland, Ohio, and

Jacksonville, Florida. The northernmost parts of Saskatchewan have a short summer, with perhaps ninety frost-free days and the first fall frost often in mid-August. A few summer days may have temperatures reaching into the 90s F (low 30s C) although the average is typically in the high 50s F (mid-10s C). Like the south it is relatively dry, with much of the north averaging less than an inch of precipitation per

■ Saskatchewan's Extreme Weather

Saskatchewan experiences fewer tornadoes than the "tornado alley" of Ontario, but in June 1912 Regina was struck by the most deadly tornado in Canadian history. For three terrifying minutes the "Regina Cyclone" swept through the city's downtown core and raked some of its more exclusive neighborhoods, leaving twenty-eight people dead and hundreds more injured. The tornado destroyed or damaged more than five hundred buildings and caused $4 million worth of property damage.

Massive thunderstorm clouds that can form on the prairies have also caused memorable storms. One famous fifteen-inch (thirty-eight-centimeter) rainstorm in Parkman in southeastern Saskatchewan in August 1985 turned a wheat field into an instant lake that a pair of brothers water-skied on. Saskatchewan's severe thunderstorms have also yielded world-class hailstorms, including one in which egg-sized hailstones piled up more than twelve feet (four meters) deep in places. Another storm near Cedoux in southeastern Saskatchewan dropped Canada's largest hailstone, a softball-sized monster weighing in at more than half a pound (one-quarter kilogram).

■ *Before and after photos of one downtown Regina building show the devasting effects of the city's 1912 tornado.*

month. "Our coldest days," notes a government website, "are often our most beautiful days, with sun dogs [bright spots on a halo around the sun] blazing in the sky and frost shining on every surface. Often on winter nights the dancing northern lights appear."[4]

Rich in Natural Resources

Saskatchewan can thank its early geologic history for its current mining and energy industries. As the huge, salt-rich inland sea that dominated the area for hundreds of millions of years gradually evaporated, it left behind beds of minerals that are now buried thousands of feet below the surface. Among these salts are a number of potassium compounds, especially potassium chloride (also known as sylvite), that are the source of the commercial fertilizer product called potash, the third most important crop nutrient after nitrogen and phosphate.

The province's ancient geologic history is also responsible for its wealth of energy resources. As the lush plant life that existed when the area was more hot and humid gradually died and decayed, over eons of time it formed the energy deposits Saskatchewan now exploits as oil, natural gas, and coal. Saskatchewan's nineteen thousand oil wells make it Canada's second-largest producer of crude oil, after Alberta. Much of the oil and natural gas exploration is concentrated in the slice of the province south of a line from Lloydminster to Estevan. The provincial government controls approximately 75 percent of oil and gas rights in Saskatchewan. Trucks, trains, and the Enbridge (formerly Interprovincial) Pipe Line, which runs through Regina, transport about three-fifths of Saskatchewan's oil to the United States.

Saskatchewan is also Canada's third-largest producer of coal, behind only Alberta and British Columbia. Saskatchewan's five open-pit coal mines are located in southern Saskatchewan. They provide the fuel for three coal-powered power plants, which provide upward of 70 percent of the province's electricity.

Human Effects on the Landscape

The human inhabitants have long had major effects on the natural landscape of what is now Saskatchewan. This was true even before the arrival of European settlers in the nineteenth

■ A World-Class Uranium Producer

Saskatchewan today produces more high-grade uranium ore than any other region in the world. Gold and copper prospectors working the northern shores of Lake Athabasca came across uranium deposits in the mid-1930s. It was not until the late 1940s that extensive uranium mining in the area began, and the town of Uranium City was established in 1952 to serve the extraction and milling facilities. By the early 1980s these mines were played out. Uranium City shriveled from a population of forty-six hundred in 1959 to two hundred today. Uranium ore deposits are currently being mined (by both underground and open-pit methods) at Rabbit Lake, Key Lake, and Cluff Lake, all in the Canadian Shield area between Reindeer Lake and Lake Athabasca. The ore is processed to provide the uranium used to fuel nuclear power plants in Canada and elsewhere. (Saskatchewan does not have any nuclear power plants—its electricity is generated by coal-fired, hydroelectric, and natural gas plants.)

■ *Canada's Uranium Resources stamp, issued in 1980, features a molecular model of the uranium-bearing mineral uraninite.*

century. For example, anthropologists say that various Indian tribes made extensive use of prairie fires to create an environment that favored their hunting-gathering lifestyle.

The changes that have occurred over the past two centuries, however, have been more dramatic than those of the previous two millennia. Saskatchewan's native grasslands have been tilled and farmed, its rivers dammed, its forests logged. The factor that quickened settlement and development in the early 1800s was the existence of seemingly limitless numbers of two animals in particular—the beaver and the buffalo.

The Lure of Beaver and Buffalo

The earliest inhabitants of present-day Saskatchewan are thought to have been nomadic bands who hunted now-extinct animals such as mammoths and giant sloths more than ten thousand years ago. As the most recent continental ice sheet melted and retreated from the northern edge of the region, stone-age societies also hunted giant bison, ancestors of the buffalo that eventually dominated the Great Plains. Over the next five millennia, the forests and woodlands that emerged in the north provided hunting grounds for nomadic societies that depended on deer, elk, and other game for their food and clothing.

Within the past three thousand years, the numerous First Nations societies of modern times, with their distinctive arts, crafts, ceremonies, and culture, slowly developed in various parts of present-day Saskatchewan. By the time European fur traders began to filter into the area in the early 1700s, the main tribes were distinguished by cultures adapted to either the forests and woodlands of the north or the prairies of the south. Numerous tribes competed for dominance within these areas. For example, among the prominent northern tribes were Chipewyan and Woodland Cree. Plains tribes included those who spoke Algonquian languages, like the Blackfoot and the Plains Cree, as well as Assiniboine and Dakota that spoke Sioux-family languages.

The arrival of European explorers and fur traders in the early eighteenth century set in motion a series of momentous changes for native societies over the next three centuries. A land and people that had evolved slowly over thousands of years was to be rocked by the rise and fall of the beaver- and buffalo-based trading economy.

Woodland and Plains Indians

The northern woodland tribes in general were hunter-trappers who often depended upon caribou, deer, moose, elk, or reindeer for food and shelter. The Chipewyans of this region, for example, "followed the migrating caribou north to the barren-grounds during the summer and south into the forest in the winter," notes archaeologist David Meyer. "It is likely that this basic subsistence-settlement pattern was established by the first human occupants of this area."[5] These societies relied to a lesser extent on other food sources as well, including small animals, fish and waterfowl, and plant foods such as roots and nuts.

Northern woodland natives were grouped into bands made up of an extended family of a dozen or more persons, most related by blood or marriage. A number of bands might have come together briefly to form a larger tribe when their prey migrated during the spring or fall.

The First Nations of the plains depended heavily on the buffalo until its near extermination in the late nineteenth century. Prior to acquiring horses, bands of plains Indians used dogs to pull a travois (a webbed frame between two poles) to transport their belongings as they followed huge buffalo herds. The people lived in small bands and developed effective communal hunting tactics that involved herding large numbers of buffalo into pounds, where they could be killed with lance or bow-and-arrow, or running herds of buffalo off of cliffs. Indians made tepees from stitched-together buffalo hides and fashioned the skins into clothing, though other animal hides such as antelope and deer were also used. The tribes preserved buffalo meat by making it into pemmican, a mixture of fat, dried meat, and berries.

The arrival of horses circa 1750 transformed plains society. As an Indian and Northern Affairs Canada report notes, "Within 100 years following its introduction, the horse was an essential part of Plains First Nations culture, whether in hunting, warfare, travel or transportation of goods."[6] The horse allowed for greater gathering of material goods and a much-expanded hunting territory. First Nations tribes could more easily accumulate stocks of food large enough to support encampments of a thousand or more persons during the summer.

Some tribes made the transition from woodland to plains society during relatively recent times. For example, bands of Woodland Cree filtered westward from eastern Canada as partners with the English and the French in the fur trade. Cree that eventually arrived in the area of present-day Saskatchewan as late as the mid-1700s gradually transformed their woodland traditions to become Plains Cree. Other woodland bands were forced westward just to survive as overhunting reduced the numbers of large game animals once abundant in eastern Canada.

For Love of the Beaver

The fur trade had a major impact not only on native societies of the northern plains but also on most of Canada's European settlers. Indeed much of Canadian history has been dictated by Europeans' love of beaver pelts, obtained from the second-largest rodent in the world (after the South American capybara). In the late 1600s beaver thrived in the millions from coast to coast in North America. The beaver that were native to Europe, on the other hand, were close to being wiped out by overtrapping. Europeans valued beaver pelts for their dense fur, from which tailors made felt. This soft and luxurious cloth

■ *Saskatchewan's now-diminished buffalo population was once a plentiful resource for the province's native population.*

became much sought after for use in fashionable hats, capes, and other items.

The Hudson's Bay Company was the first of numerous enterprises that would seek to exploit North America's seemingly limitless supply of beaver. England's King Charles II granted a group of London merchants a charter in 1670 to both establish a fur trading company and to explore the unknown northern reaches of the New World. The charter covered the huge tract of land that came to be known as Rupert's Land (named after a royal cousin), including the entire area drained by the rivers that flow into the Hudson Bay. The Hudson's Bay Company wasted little time and soon had trading posts established at promising sites where major east-flowing rivers, such as the Nelson and Hayes, emptied into the southwestern part of the Hudson Bay.

The first Europeans to visit the region that we now know as Saskatchewan were thus fur traders. The earliest exploration occurred in 1690 when Henry Kelsey of the Hudson's Bay Company made a two-year reconnaissance of the lake-strewn north. He led a party including native guides up the Hayes River in canoes from York Factory, the company's chief port on the Hudson Bay. The Kelsey expedition crossed present-day Manitoba and connected up with the Saskatchewan River. It reached the area of present-day Saskatoon and ventured, at times overland, possibly as far as present-day southern Alberta. The party returned to York Factory in the summer of 1692. Kelsey's journal describes the plains, animals

■ *Beavers thrive both in forested areas and along tree-lined prairie streams. The dense brown fur of a single large adult was enough to make more than a dozen fur hats.*

including buffalo and grizzly bears, and his encounter with a tribe of Sioux or Gros Ventres.

The Hudson's Bay Company was somewhat slow to follow up on Kelsey's findings. Rather than establishing inland posts, its early strategy was to "sit by the Bay" and encourage natives and traders to bring furs to its ports. First Nations traders spread European goods to woodland tribes many decades before whites arrived in person. It was not until 1754 that the company sent trader Anthony Henday down the North Saskatchewan River almost all the way to its source in the Rockies.

The Hudson's Bay Company's lack of initiative left an opening in the fur trade that the French quickly exploited. The French had established colonies in Quebec and explored the area of the St. Lawrence River by the mid-1600s. Much like Charles II, the late–seventeenth century French king Louis XIV took steps to promote the fur trade. Lacking ports on the Hudson Bay, French traders began to build a series of fur-trading posts on rivers and lakes in the Great Lakes region, gradually expanding farther west. The French encouraged trappers to intermarry with native women, and it is the descendants of these early unions that make up the Métis (French for "mixed") people who were to play a crucial role in

■ *An artist imaginatively reconstructs the scene of young Henry Kelsey first encountering plains bison during his 1690–1692 expedition for the Hudson's Bay Company.*

Saskatchewan history. By the 1730s the French fur trader Pierre La Vérendrye had established a number of fur-trading posts in present-day southern Ontario and Manitoba. Expeditions that he, his sons, and a nephew undertook reached as far as the fork of the North and South Saskatchewan rivers. Trading posts the French established along the Saskatchewan River in the 1740s were the earliest European settlements in what developed into Saskatchewan.

After British forces defeated the French in 1759 at a battle on the Plains of Abraham outside Quebec City, the French were forced to relinquish control of their Canadian colonies. French fur traders and soldiers began to abandon forts they had set up as far west as present-day central Saskatchewan. By the 1770s the Hudson's Bay Company had slowly infiltrated the heartland of the country. Its earliest inland post was Cumberland House, named after the duke of Cumberland. It was built on the banks of the Saskatchewan River, near the present Manitoba border, by the Hudson's Bay Company explorer Samuel Hearne in 1774. Cumberland House is now the oldest nonnative continuously occupied site in Saskatchewan.

■ *Cumberland House was built as part of the Hudson's Bay Company's effort to extend the fur trade inland during the late eighteenth century.*

The Free-Spirited North West Company

The Hudson's Bay Company faced a new competitor in the fur trade when a group of Scottish, British, and French fur

traders and merchants formed the Montreal-based North West Company in the 1780s. The North West Company took over some of the posts and forts abandoned by the French and encouraged its traders to expand westward. The North West Company readily worked with First Nations groups to boost the fur trade, a partnership that had for native society both pros (acquisition of Western tools, from guns to iron cooking pots) and cons (exposure to alcohol and to deadly European-introduced diseases such as smallpox).

The North West Company was particularly keen on finding a river route to the Pacific. By the 1790s it had established a number of posts on the Saskatchewan River, which was increasingly recognized as a major fur-trading artery of the twelve hundred-mile (two thousand-kilometer) canoe route from the Hudson Bay all the way to the Rockies. From where the Saskatchewan empties into Cedar Lake in present-day Manitoba, fur traders could also travel southeast to reach the Great Lakes and the commercial centers of Toronto and Montreal. And with occasional portages, traders could link up with Reindeer Lake and points north.

Many of the great western explorers in Canadian history were thus North West Company employees who traveled through parts of present-day Saskatchewan as they sought viable transcontinental routes. Among the most notable was David Thompson, the preeminent North West Company geographer who mapped more than 1 million square miles (2.6 million square kilometers) of land during journeys taken from 1785 to 1812. He crisscrossed present-day Saskatchewan a number of times, reaching as far north as Lake Athabasca and as far south as the North Saskatchewan River.

After a decade of increasingly bloody confrontations between the Hudson's Bay and North West companies, the two merged in 1821. Despite the merger, over the next few decades the trade in beaver fur declined. The extensive trapping over the past century had begun to take its toll on the beaver population and beaver hats were no longer so fashionable in Europe. (Beaver in Canada have fully recovered and today approach the carrying capacity of the land in many places.) The buffalo, on the other hand, still seemed to be inexhaustible in supply, though the largest herds were west of the Assiniboine River of present-day Manitoba. The seminomadic, buffalo-pursuing lifestyle of Métis traders pushed many of them into the plains of present-day Saskatchewan.

Surveying the Prairies

As it became clear that beaver were not the limitless resource once thought, both the British government and the province of Canada (now Ontario and Quebec) became more interested in finding out about the cultures, animals, and plants of the area, as well as exploring transcontinental routes. The Hudson's Bay Company, which still maintained political if not economic control over Rupert's Land, remained lukewarm about agricultural settlement. One company official claimed, for example, that the "poverty of the soil"[7] prevented settlement except along riverbanks. Many government officials, however, saw the prairies as a potentially vast farmland. What was needed more than anything else was information.

In the mid-1850s the London Royal Geographical Society, with help from the Hudson's Bay Company, agreed to fund an expedition to explore and survey the Canadian prairies. Led by the Irish-born adventurer John Palliser, the expedition eventually filed its report in 1863. Palliser discovered the existence of a huge arid region, now known as Palliser's Triangle,

■ The Palliser Expedition

In the late 1840s John Palliser had gone on a year-long buffalo-hunting expedition in the American West. He wrote a popular book about his experiences and searched for an opportunity to return. The fact-finding expedition to the area north of the 49th parallel, the border between the United States and British-controlled Canada, fit the bill perfectly. Palliser sailed from England in 1857 and hoped to return eighteen months later. Guided by a Métis and accompanied by naturalists with expertise in geology, botany, and astronomy, Palliser ended up spending three years trekking through the southern and central sections of present-day Saskatchewan, Alberta, and British Columbia.

In addition to evaluating the land's agricultural potential and developing a detailed map of the area, Palliser's company reached the Rockies and identified a half-dozen passes that might accommodate a transcontinental railroad. One of these, Kicking Horse Pass, was used when the Canadian Pacific Railway built the railroad in the mid-1880s.

Palliser's reports on the area's wildlife were also notable. *The Papers of the Palliser Expedition, 1857–1860* includes a description of a massive herd of buffalo that "sounded like the roar of distant rapids in a large river, and [caused] a vibration also something like a trembling in the ground."

in present-day southwestern Saskatchewan and southeastern Alberta. He said that the lack of rainfall there made it generally unpromising for farming. He also reported, however, that a fertile parkland belt just north of this triangle was suitable for farms or cattle ranches.

Palliser's comments, notes a University of Calgary report, were encouraging to Canadians seeking to expand the country's borders, who "found the discussion of a fertile belt enticing, as it bolstered their desire to annex the region."[8] Palliser's conclusions at the time also reinforced the findings of another, less ambitious expedition that overlapped his. This one had been funded by Britain and the Canadian colony and led by Henry Youle Hind, a professor of chemistry and geology at the University of Trinity College, Toronto. Like Palliser, Hind found a "fertile belt" that extended from about present-day Winnipeg to Edmonton. Hind's report crowed that "no other part of North America [has] this singularly favourable disposition of soil and climate."[9]

These surveys also came at an opportune time for supporters of Canadian independence. In the mid-1860s the provinces of Canada, Nova Scotia, and New Brunswick began to consider merging to form a new country. With the approval of the British Parliament, the Dominion of Canada was born in 1867, with the former province of Canada being split into the provinces of Quebec and Ontario. A major issue for the new country was the status of the sprawling lands still held by the Hudson's Bay Company, including much of present-day Saskatchewan. In 1870 Canada purchased this mostly unpopulated land from the company and immediately began to consider how to promote rapid settlement.

■ *John Palliser's 1857–1860 expedition provided important new information about the prairies and mountains of western North America.*

The Cypress Hills Massacre

The new country's "North-West Territories" was a wild and unruly place in the early 1870s, especially in the areas closest to the border with the United States. American fur traders operating out of Montana were discovering that it was more profitable to sell guns and whiskey to the Black-foot and Assiniboine than to peddle buffalo robes. The illegal whiskey trade even had its own routes, dotted with forts like Fort Whoop-Up in what is now southern Alberta. The whiskey trade had devastating effects on the native culture. According to an 1875 report by the British War Office, the "demoralizing sale of liquor and arms" led to eighty-eight Blackfoot being murdered in brawls in 1871 alone. The report noted:

> Murderers go about at large openly; there have been hith-erto no means and therefore no attempt to enforce law; and the land is infested with filibusters [military adventurers] and outlaws from the United States who carry on this illicit trade in contraband goods with the Indians, whom they also rob and defraud. With these they often have quarrels, and the grossest outrages are committed.[10]

■ The Mounties' Centennial Museum and Depot

In 1920 the Canadian government merged the North-West Mounted Police with the Dominion Police to form the Royal Canadian Mounted Police (RCMP) and moved the force's headquarters from Regina to Ottawa. The world-famous Mounties nevertheless remains an important institution in Saskatchewan. Regina is the site of the RCMP Centennial Museum and its eclectic collection of more than thirty thousand artifacts, weapons, uniforms, and documents. The stately RCMP Chapel, built as a mess hall in 1883, is Regina's oldest building.

While the Centennial Museum honors the force's past, the nearby Depot Division training academy serves the present. Visitors are welcome to tour the facility, where each year some five hundred cadets undergo six months of rigorous training. Visitors can also peer into a state-of-the-art forensic lab or watch ceremonial events such as the Sergeant Major's Parade. During the summer, a once-a-week evening flag-lowering ceremony, conducted by smartly dressed Mounties, always draws a large crowd.

■ *Constable Jeff Ellis, astride "General," wears the ceremonial red uniform of the Royal Canadian Mounted Police.*

The violence and lawlessness of the whiskey trade reached a climax in July 1873 near Battle Creek in the Cypress Hills. A dozen or so wolfers (wolf hunters who often killed wolves by poisoning the carcasses of dead buffalo) accused a band of Assiniboine of stealing their horses. After a night of heavy drinking, the wolfers—mostly Americans but also a few Canadians and Métis—tracked the Assiniboine to an encampment. When a tense negotiation failed, the wolfers opened fire on the camp from the protection of a gully. The wolfers, unlike the Indians, were armed with the latest repeating rifles, and Indian warriors who tried to charge the entrenched position were easily cut down. The incident left as many as three dozen Indians dead—historians are unsure of the exact toll—along with one wolfer.

The Cypress Hills Massacre, as the press dubbed it, caused a public outcry in Canada. The American West had a reputation for violence, gunplay, and the slaughter of native tribes that Canada did not wish to emulate. The fact that Americans were not only profiteering through the whiskey trade but crossing the border to engage in one-sided gun battles with Indians was seen as an affront to Canadian authority. The federal government put plans for a federal police force on the fast track and by August 1873 had finalized the formation of the North-West Mounted Police.

By the summer of 1874 the government had recruited and trained a force of almost three hundred mounted police and dispatched it to the prairies of present-day Saskatchewan and Alberta. Units operating out of Fort Walsh were unable to find and apprehend those guilty of the previous summer's massacre, but Mountie presence in the territory was a major factor in ending the whiskey trade. First Nations tribes, initially wary of putting any trust in this government force, eventually recognized the Mounties as allies who could be useful in protecting native rights and supervising treaties.

Slow to Settle

In addition to establishing law and order, Canada also sought to rapidly promote settlement in its new territory. In 1872 the federal government passed the Dominion Lands Act, which promised 160 acres (65 hectares) free to settlers at least twenty-one years old. For their part, the settlers had to pay a small registration fee, promise to live on the land for three years, cultivate at least thirty acres (twelve hectares), and build a permanent dwelling.

In spite of the Lands Act, people were slow to flock to Canada's prairie heartland. One problem was a lingering perception that much of the land was too arid to farm. Basic amenities, such as wood and water, were often scarce. Many of the earliest farmers had to build not log houses but shelters of sod. "Prairie shingles" were stacked grass-side down in slabs to form walls and put on top of boards to form the roof. Another problem related to the economic depression that much of the world was mired in during the 1870s. The demand, and thus the prices, for crops like wheat were low. It took a number of developments in the 1880s, including the building of the transcontinental railroad, to brighten the future for this part of the western prairies.

Birth of Saskatchewan and Regina

The North-West Territories, which had been established as a distinct political unit of the infant country in 1876, was in 1882 divided south of the 60th parallel into four new districts. The District of Assiniboia encompassed much of present-day prairie Saskatchewan, while the District of Saskatchewan, named after the river, encompassed much of the remainder of the lower half of present-day Saskatchewan. The District of Alberta was to the west. To the north was the District of Athabasca, which included much of the northern half of present-day Saskatchewan.

When Canada established these new districts, it also relocated the seat of the North-West Territories' government from Battleford to Regina. The decision to move the capital was made by the territorial lieutenant-governor, who consulted with the Canadian Pacific Railway (which planned to go through Regina) and Canada's first prime minister, John Macdonald. According to a Legislative Assembly of Alberta history, "Many citizens were upset by this decision. It was alleged that the Lieutenant-Governor was motivated by the fact that he owned property in Regina."[11]

The choice of Regina was controversial in part because it was then nothing but a tiny tent settlement on the banks of the Wascana Creek. Wascana is a transliteration of the Cree word *oskana,* which literally means "pile of bones." The site had earned this name by being the place on the creek where native tribes butchered their buffalo catch and left what they could not use—mostly the bones. The federal government obviously saw the need for a more sophisticated name for the new capital of the North-West Territories. It settled upon Regina, from the Latin for queen, as a tribute to honor England's Queen Victoria, then approaching the golden anniversary of what would become a sixty-four-year reign.

The Northwest Rebellion of 1885

One last major obstacle remained to the rapid development of the area: simmering political discontent among the aboriginal (First Nations and Métis) population over land issues and treaty promises. White settlers in the Battleford area were angry as well about political decisions that deprived them of the government capital and the railroad. In 1885 the widespread dissatisfaction erupted into the violent Northwest Rebellion, which took place on land that is now Saskatchewan.

First Nations tribes under the leadership of the Cree chiefs Big Bear (Mistahimaskwa) and Poundmaker (Pitikwahanapiwiyin), Blackfoot chief Crowfoot (Isapo-Muxika), and others were failing to thrive on the reserves assigned them by treaties. The Canadian government had hoped plains tribes would become farmers, but the land was arid and bands began to starve. When First Nations chiefs' pleas for help were ignored by the government in the early 1880s, various plains Indians groups considered forming a coalition to increase their collective power.

The Métis felt similarly slighted by the federal government. They had received little government help or even recognition as a people during the decade after the establishment of Manitoba. That province, initially much smaller than today, failed to become the homeland the Métis hoped for. Pushed west, the Métis—much like the plains Indians—struggled mightily as their main resource, the buffalo, disappeared.

Métis Leader Louis Riel

The protest intensified in the spring of 1884 when the Métis invited Louis Riel, the leader of the 1870 rebellion that

■ *Métis leader Louis Riel.*

had at least briefly won the Métis a homeland in Manitoba, to return from exile in the United States. A revered figure among the Métis, Riel arrived that summer and quickly petitioned the federal government with a list of grievances. When no progress had been made by the following spring, the Métis declared a provisional government of Saskatchewan and organized an army led by the crafty outdoorsman Gabriel Dumont. The Canadian government put its troops on alert. A large Métis force struck the first blow on March 26, 1885, at Duck Lake. With the help of some natives the Métis routed a hundred or so North-West Mounted Police and citizen volunteers and caused the Mounties to abandon nearby Fort Carlton. The Métis then gathered in Batoche, a small Métis commercial center located between Prince Albert and Saskatoon, and began to fortify the town.

After Duck Lake, Cree chief Poundmaker organized a march of native men, women, and children from reserves in western present-day Saskatchewan to Fort Battleford. Poundmaker later said that his intention was to negotiate with Canadian officials and try to convince them to provide the famine relief Treaty 6 called for. By the time his group reached the area, the whites had abandoned the surrounding village and were barricaded inside the fort, fearful of an attack. The Indian agent refused to even talk with Poundmaker. The Indians turned around and went home, though a few stole food and supplies from homes in the village.

Meanwhile, the Canadian government in Ottawa responded to news of the battle at Duck Lake by mobilizing some five thousand men to confront the "traitors." Within a month the army, under the command of Major-General Frederick Middleton, was engaged in bloody skirmishes with native and Métis forces.

Defeat at Batoche

The armed rebellion lasted for three months and claimed about 125 lives. One of the rebels' most successful engagements was fought on May 2 at Cut Knife Hill, near Poundmaker's encampment. A militia lead by Lieutenant-Colonel William Otter was forced to retreat after a day-long battle that killed eight soldiers and a half-dozen natives. Poundmaker apparently remained a "peace chief," counseling against pursuing the retreating force—and probably preventing a slaughter of the white soldiers. Poundmaker could not control "war chiefs" such as Wandering Spirit (Kapapamahchakwew), however, and the Indians set off for Batoche. Their exact plans remain unclear today, as does the extent to which natives and Métis collaborated during the rebellion.

Such successes were short-lived in the face of the government's greater manpower and firepower. The rebellion's death-knell was Middleton's three-day siege of Batoche and the defeat of Riel's forces there on May 12. A native band led by Wandering Spirit continued to fight and held off a much larger government force at the Battle of Frenchman Butte in late May, but it seems that further bloodshed was recognized as futile by both sides. The rebellion's final engagements—

■ *Canadian troops wind through the Touchwood Hills north of Qu'Appelle on their way to quelling the Northwest Rebellion of 1885.*

■ Cree Chief Poundmaker

Poundmaker was born in the early 1840s in west-central present-day Saskatchewan, son of a Stoney shaman and a Cree-Métis mother. Poundmaker's name refers to an important native skill, the building of a pound or corral that would be used during a communal hunt to capture herds of buffalo. After both of his parents died while Poundmaker was still young, he was raised by a Red Pheasant Cree band near North Battleford. Poundmaker developed into a skillful hunter and became a chief in 1878. Intelligent and articulate, he was considered a visionary leader who demanded respect from government officials and worked hard to get the best treaty terms for his people. One such clause in Treaty 6, requiring the Canadian government to feed his people during periods of famine, would play a role in the Northwest Rebellion of 1885.

Following Riel's defeat at Batoche, Poundmaker was quickly arrested and charged with treason-felony. Despite Poundmaker's statement that "I can't understand how it is that after saving so many lives I am brought here," he was tried and found guilty. After serving less than one year of his three-year sentence, Poundmaker was released due to poor health. He died at age forty-four only a few weeks later. An editorial in the *Regina Leader* after Poundmaker's death seemed to acknowledge the injustice done him: "A man with a large, generous heart, the nobleness of his nature was written on his lofty and handsome face. . . . He was a born leader of his people. A great man has fallen and we pay him, with genuine regret and respect, this last tribute."

Poundmaker's legacy is honored in a number of ways in Saskatchewan today, perhaps most notably at the Chief Poundmaker Historical Centre and Teepee Village located on the Poundmaker Reserve west of North Battleford. It includes various displays and artifacts from the life of a man who was widely admired by friends and adversaries alike.

■ *The powerful Cree chieftain Poundmaker poses with one of his three wives.*

indeed the last military battles on Canadian soil—took place in early June 1885. A small detachment of the North-West Mounted Police tracked some of Wandering Spirit's warriors, and their hostages from Fort Pitt, to Loon Lake. After a short gun battle with minor casualties, the natives took off northward with their prisoners, who later escaped or were released. The Mounties did not pursue the warriors and, a few days later, when Middleton's forces could not find the rebels, the Northwest Rebellion sputtered to a close.

Canada brought charges against 127 natives and Métis for their rebellion. Big Bear was tried and found guilty of treason-felony. Like Poundmaker, he served only a part of his three-year sentence before being released in poor health and dying a short time later. Eight other natives, including Wandering Spirit, were less fortunate—they were convicted of murder (most for an attack on whites at Frog Lake in the first week of hostilities) and hanged. Dumont fled the country, although he later returned to Batoche, where his death in 1906 was barely mentioned in the local papers. He has since been resurrected as a Canadian hero, the subject of books and movies. This is true also of Louis Riel, who was tried in Regina for high treason as the instigator of the Northwest Rebellion. By the end of November 1885, he had been found guilty, hanged, and buried in St. Boniface, Manitoba.

Preparing for Provincehood

The Northwest Rebellion remains a controversial topic in Saskatchewan, with many natives and Métis still viewing it as a justified protest. The Cree note that even the name reflects cultural perceptions—they refer to the Northwest Resistance rather than the Northwest Rebellion. It is commemorated at various sites, including Batoche, where battle trenches and a church with bullet holes over its doorway remain a visible reminder of turbulent times.

In the wake of the Northwest Rebellion, the Canadian government had its hands full for another two decades trying to establish law and order in the area. Most of the worst lawlessness occurred in the south, where the Big Muddy Badlands offered a haven for such western outlaws as Butch Cassidy and Sam Kelley. Criminals would steal horses in Montana and then cross the border into Saskatchewan District, knowing that

American lawmen would not pursue them. Until almost the turn of the century the many deep gullies and caves of the badlands prevented the Mounties from scattering most of these outlaws.

By then Saskatchewan was on the verge of officially becoming a province. Canada's department of the interior was also implementing an ambitious settlement plan that would begin to transform Saskatchewan from a frontier area to a pioneer society of homesteaders, farmers, ranchers, and merchants.

A Cooperative Tradition

Western Canada developed quickly at the turn of the century, in the wake of Wilfrid Laurier's election as prime minister of Canada in 1896. Laurier recognized that the North-West Territories were becoming increasingly difficult to govern. Residents in Saskatchewan and the other districts were bombarding Ottawa with requests for increased local power, greater representation in the federal government, and authority to tax railway properties. Laurier's government considered making the territory into a single new province but feared the political and economic clout such a superprovince might hold. After much political infighting among Laurier's ruling Liberal Party and its Conservative Party opponents, the Autonomy Bills of 1905 created two new provinces, Alberta and Saskatchewan. Laurier divided the land so that the provinces would be approximately equal in size and population. (The population of Alberta has since grown to almost triple that of Saskatchewan.)

The federal government retained control of the land, natural resources, and royalties from timber and other sales within the new provincial boundaries. This slight—all the previously admitted provinces were benefiting economically from their land and other resources—would be a source of western resentment toward Ottawa until 1930, when the federal government finally reversed its decision.

Control of the land was crucial to the federal government because of its intention to promote immigration to the west. Laurier appointed the energetic Clifford Sifton as minister of the interior, and he immediately put into action various plans

for attracting newcomers who would take up farming. Sifton streamlined the immigration process, pressured the railways to stop hoarding the best land, and published pamphlets in various languages to extol life on the prairies. The diverse immigrants who arrived began to band together for protection from political and economic forces based in eastern Canada, eventually leading to a tradition of provincial concern for the welfare of all citizens, rich and poor, young and old.

Who Needs "Gentleman Emigrants"?

Sifton was unafraid to challenge conventional thinking about what types of immigrants were desirable. Canada had previously focused on "keeping Canada British" but Sifton expanded the depart-

■ *As federal minister of the interior from 1896 to 1905, Clifford Sifton directed an aggressive campaign to settle the western plains.*

ment's net to draw in more people from the United States and Europe. Many Canadian officials feared that an influx of Americans would encourage the U.S. government to try to annex part of the Canadian prairies. Sifton recognized that many immigrants from south of the border were experienced farmers who often brought considerable capital with them. "Sifton's campaign to attract American farmers was so effective," notes Canada's Citizenship and Immigration department, "that Americans constituted the largest group of immigrant settlers in the provinces of Saskatchewan and Alberta when they were created in 1905."[12]

Even more controversial among many Canadians than encouraging immigration from the United States were efforts to attract more eastern and central Europeans, such as Germans and people from the Austro-Hungarian provinces of Galicia and Bukovina (now mostly Ukraine). Sifton thought that these sturdy peasants would be more likely than the "gentleman emigrants" from London, for example, to work hard, succeed at farming, and have lots of children. Ultimately, as many as 170,000 Ukrainians settled in Canada between 1890 and the outbreak of World War I, often in the rolling, semi-wooded parkland belt of the prairie provinces that reminded them of the landscapes they had left behind in central Europe.

After 1910 an anti-ethnic backlash began to change the face of prairie settlement. A head tax was instituted to allow only the richest Chinese to settle in Canada. Black Americans trying to immigrate to Saskatchewan and Alberta (mainly from Oklahoma) faced informal rules and ploys that stemmed the moderate numbers of the previous decade.

The New Province Prospers

Saskatchewan's first decade as a province was one of population growth and economic success. Settlers like the Métis, Ukrainians, and others from eastern Canada, the United States, and Europe helped to establish farming and ranching in the southern half of Saskatchewan. The cities of Regina and Saskatoon boomed on speculative land deals. Land investment companies published ads, maps, and pamphlets that promised easy money to newcomers. One 1907 map, for example, extolled Saskatoon as "the city of unlimited possibilities" and "the centre of the British Empire."[13] Settlement and economic growth resulted in huge increases in population for Saskatchewan. By 1911 Saskatchewan had become Canada's

■ *British settlers on their way to founding the city of Lloydminster set up a temporary tent camp in Saskatoon in 1903.*

third-largest province. A decade later its population peaked at almost a million people, a figure it would barely surpass over the next eighty years.

Much of Saskatchewan's early success was due to its ability to establish itself as the breadbasket of the world, capable of exporting millions of bushels of wheat every year. This development was only possible, however, after much hard work and innovation by the province's farmers. As late as the 1890s, farming Canada's prairie heartland was still a risky business. In some areas as many as three in every four farmers were failing completely. Farming in Saskatchewan began to reach its potential only after a number of crucial developments. For example, advances in irrigation included widespread use of dugouts, small, private reservoirs that can hold a million or more gallons of water. Just as important were changes in how farmers grew wheat on the northern plains and what type of wheat was grown.

A healthy dose of the credit for Saskatchewan's growth as "the breadbasket province" goes to William Motherwell, a modest man sometimes called the "Grand Old Man of Canadian Agriculture." He was one of the few farmers drawn to the plains in the late nineteenth century who was college-trained in agriculture. A learned and observant man, Mother-

■ *An early steam-powered tractor plows through the rich soil of the Canadian Plains.*

■ The Grand Old Man of Canadian Agriculture

William Motherwell was born on a farm in Perth, Canada West (present-day Ontario), in 1860. Shortly after becoming one of the first graduates of the Ontario Agricultural College in 1882, Motherwell decided to take up the government's offer of free homesteading land in the prairies of the North-West Territories. He moved from Ontario to a site on the prairies about sixty miles (one hundred kilometers) east of Regina. He built a sod cabin, bought some farm tools and animals, and planted his fields. One of his most successful crops was an unusual variety of grass that yielded valuable seeds, which he sold to other farmers. After a decade the rural community of Abernethy began to take hold nearby and Motherwell was successful enough to build an impressive house and grounds for his family.

After two decades of farming, Motherwell went on to become a leading political figure in both provincial and federal farming policy. In 1901 he was one of the cofounders and early leaders of the Territorial (later Saskatchewan) Grain Growers' Association, which fought the railway monopoly and lobbied for lower tariffs. When Saskatchewan became a province, he served for thirteen years as its first minister of agriculture.

The public's growing respect for Motherwell caused two prime ministers to tap him to serve as the federal minister of agriculture between 1921 and 1930. Among the reforms he lobbied for were national measures to increase farm production. In the 1930s he founded a research facility concerned with prairie cultivation and new varieties of wheat. Prior to his death in 1943 in Regina, he may have relished most the comment of a Yorkton banker who was quoted in 1941 as saying, according to Agriculture and Agri-Food Canada's profile of Motherwell, "He has been in politics for many years, but during all those years he has always been regarded as a good farmer, even among his neighbours; and this is the acid test."

The estatelike homestead that Motherwell built over many years in Abernethy is now a national historic site and a popular tourist attraction. The ten rooms in the Italianate-style stone farmhouse have been restored with original furnishings circa 1910, and the carefully arranged settings and vintage accessories make it look like the Motherwell family might walk through the front door at any time. During the summer, the facility is staffed by more than a dozen guides in period costumes who bake bread, do chores, and care for the landscaped grounds and the farm animals.

well pondered the reasons why so many of his neighbors were failing and having to abandon their new farms. Motherwell realized that a number of the farming techniques being used locally were imports from Ontario or places in the United States where more rain fell and the growing season was longer. Motherwell experimented with techniques more appropriate for the cooler and more arid northern prairies, such as leaving a field fallow every other year to let it recover moisture and nutrients. He became a strong advocate for "dry-land farming" techniques as well as for other innovations, including planting "shelterbelt" rows of trees to break the wind and reduce soil erosion.

The other major factor that promoted the success of prairie farming was a change in the type of wheat being grown. Wheat had been grown in western Canada since at least 1812, when a group of mostly Scottish immigrant farmers organized by Thomas Douglas, fifth earl of Selkirk, established the Red River Colony south of Lake Winnipeg, in present-day Manitoba. Yields were generally poor, however, until the early 1840s, when Ontario farmer David Fife began to plant a strain of Ukrainian spring wheat that could grow more quickly during the short, relatively dry growing seasons of the northern plains. (Spring wheats are planted in the spring and harvested in the fall; winter wheats, which are planted in the fall and harvested in the spring, do not do well in cold Saskatchewan.) What came to be known as Red Fife (red referring to the color of the wheat kernel) achieved wide popularity on the prairies. In the first decade of the twentieth century, Canadian researchers used Red Fife to develop a new wheat variety called Marquis that was even better suited to the prairie provinces. Marquis, notes wheat historian Stephan Symko, "attracted attention in every wheat-growing country because of the surprisingly high quality of its grain and flour, its early ripening (several days earlier than Red Fife), high yield, and the fact that its straw does not lie flat. The introduction of Marquis was the greatest practical triumph of Canadian agriculture."[14] In combination with dry-land farming techniques, Marquis allowed wheat farming to skyrocket from 8 million bushels in 1896 to 232 million bushels by 1912.

A Province with a Social Conscience

During this time Saskatchewan developed a political and social conscience that has remained a distinctive trait to this day. For example, women won the vote in Saskatchewan in 1916, two years before Canada granted all women the vote. The government of Saskatchewan also helped to establish the Federation of Saskatchewan Indian Nations, one of the first such native political organizations in Canada. Discontent with the seemingly probusiness policies of eastern, industrial Canada sowed the seeds for western labor parties that represented the interests of working men and women.

This early political and social concern was also evident in Saskatchewan's distinctive co-op movement. In part this may have been due to the large number of British immigrants who settled in rural Saskatchewan both before and after the backlash against ethnic immigrants around 1910. As historian Nelson Wiseman notes in "The Pattern of Prairie Politics," the British brought over "a socialist, labourist and agrarian heritage which stressed the abolition of a competitive system and the substitution of a cooperative system of manufacturing, transportation and distribution."[15]

According to Simon Fraser University political scientist David Laycock:

> Of all Canada's regions, the West participated most enthusiastically in the new era of democracy from 1900 to 1930. By 1905, all three prairie provinces had grain growers' associations which acted as farmers' lobby groups and effectively dealt with private grain companies, the world grain trade, financial institutions, and railways. As one-member, one-vote enterprises, co-operatives allowed farmers to manage their economic affairs in their own communities, while developing experience in democratic decision-making. This made it easier for farmers to think creatively about alternative political practices and policies.[16]

During the first decades of the twentieth century, pro-farming political parties as well as a host of nonprofit producer cooperatives formed to promote the sale of grain and livestock. The member-controlled co-op organizations used joint marketing and handling business practices to gain greater economic control for individual farmers. Among the most prominent co-ops was the Saskatchewan Wheat Pool begun in 1924. Farmers formed it, notes a provincial history, because they "were still convinced that the system of wheat marketing left the farmer at the mercy of the grain elevators, the large milling concerns, and the speculators."[17] The Wheat Pool eventually grew into a publicly traded company and one of the largest grain handlers in Canada. Farmers also organized to form the Saskatchewan Cooperative Elevator Company so that they would have an alternative to the high prices being charged by some private grain elevators.

By the late 1920s, however, the growing social awareness within the young province was accompanied by subtle signs of economic distress. In some years Saskatchewan's farmers grew so much wheat and other grains that supply overtook demand, causing prices to fall. Many farmers borrowed large amounts of money to expand their business. The danger of having an economy overly dependent upon the farming sector was to become all too clear when the world plummeted into the Great Depression of the 1930s.

The "Dirty Decade"

The 1930s were tough for all the people of North America but were even more disastrous for the people of Saskatchewan. The Great Depression hit the western provinces especially hard because of their reliance on exports of grains and natural resources such as lumber and minerals. As exports shriveled up, jobs disappeared and banks and businesses failed. In Saskatchewan, the combination of crop failures, plummeting wheat exports, and rock-bottom grain prices put upward of two out of three rural residents out of work. The province's total income fell by 90 percent within two years. As W.E. Garrett noted:

> Triggered by the crash of 1929, depression stalked the prairies for years, with nature as a partner. For almost a decade, drought, hot summers, early frosts, wheat rust, grasshopper plagues, and earth-moving winds destroyed crops and thousands of farmers. Topsoil became the west's only export. Dust clouds cast a pall over the land, and the

■ *"Bennett Buggies," horse-drawn automobiles like this one, shown in front of the University of Saskatchewan in 1935, were used by farmers who were too poor to buy gasoline during the Great Depression.*

The Regina Riot of 1935

One of the most violent riots in Canadian history occurred in Regina. During the depression the federal government had created some 150 relief camps for unemployed workers, especially those who were young, single men. (Although social reforms such as unemployment insurance had not yet been instituted, most of the provinces were at least attempting to help family groups.) The young men were put to work building roads, planting trees, and constructing public facilities in exchange for food and a one-dollar-per-week wage. The hard work and low wages soon had the men grumbling about the "slave camps." In early June 1935, more than a thousand angry camp workers in British Columbia organized a transcontinental "On to Ottawa Trek." They commandeered a fifty-boxcar freight train in Vancouver and planned to travel to the national capital and confront Canadian prime minister Richard B. Bennett with their complaints.

The trek was shaping up as a public relations disaster for the Conservative Party government. The protesters were being cheered by local crowds at train stops, and more unemployed men were joining the journey. On June 14 the train reached Regina. Bennett decided to halt the trek there and arrest the leaders, by force if necessary. While troops prevented the protesters from reboarding the train, Bennett invited eight trek leaders to meet with him in Ottawa. The two sides remained hostile and the one-hour talk on June 22 solved nothing. Trek leaders had few options left, however, and had apparently decided to disband the trek. Nevertheless, on July 1, hundreds of federal and local police stormed out of moving vans that had been parked around Regina's Market Square, the site of a final rally of some two thousand people. The resulting riot left one policeman dead and about a hundred persons injured, including forty police.

■ *Citizens scuffle with Royal Canadian Mounted Police and Regina city policemen in the "Dominion Day Riot" of July 1, 1935.*

■ "Go Slow, Aim High!": The Life of Activist Violet McNaughton

Saskatchewan's most effective agrarian feminist for much of the twentieth century was no doubt Violet McNaughton. From her roots as a Saskatchewan wheat farmer she fought for a host of political and social causes. McNaughton played a key role not only in winning women the right to vote but also in establishing Canada's national health care system.

McNaughton was born in Borden, England, in 1879. At the turn of the century she decided to emigrate to Saskatchewan to join family members living near Saskatoon. She married a struggling wheat farmer in 1910 and was soon immersed in the politics of the cooperative movement and farmers' rights. After joining the local branch of the Saskatchewan Grain Growers' Association, McNaughton saw the need for an association that could focus on issues of special concern to women, including winning women the right to vote in provincial elections. As the founder and first president of the Women Grain Growers, McNaughton rallied farm women on the prairies and beyond to "go slow, aim high!" The coalition of agrarian feminists and temperance advocates that McNaughton organized finally won women the right to vote in Saskatchewan in 1916.

After Canada granted all women the right to vote in 1918, McNaughton and the Women Grain Growers turned their attention to other issues, including the need for a publicly funded health care system. The campaign for

grit sifted into the very soul of the prairies. Weathered homes still can be found with battered utensils on the shelves and faded pictures on the walls, untouched since the owners fled.[18]

Wheat production, which had been increasing steadily since the 1880s, fell during the Dirty Thirties to two-thirds of what it had been the previous decade. The years of 1936 to 1938 were the worst, with almost thirteen thousand of the province's farms being abandoned in 1936 alone.

The low point of the Dirty Thirties for Saskatchewan was the violent Regina Riot that occurred during the summer of 1935. Prime Minister Bennett's use of troops to break up the On to Ottawa Trek prompted a government inquiry. Although it found little fault with Bennett's actions, in the eyes of much of the public the government was guilty of using violence to break up a legal and peaceful demonstration. The protest contributed to the downfall of the Conservative Party govern-

"Medical Aid Within the Reach of All" was ahead of its time, but this was essentially the model for the province's landmark system. "While men like Tommy Douglas and Emmett Hall are often credited with the birth of medicare in this country," noted CBC columnist Judy Rebick, "it was Saskatchewan women who first raised the idea. It was also farm women who took these demands into the CCF in the 1930s."

Using her biweekly "Mainly for Women" column in the influential farm journal *Western Producer* from 1925 until 1950, McNaughton took on controversial issues ranging from birth control to water pollution. By the time of her death in Saskatoon in 1968, she had made a lasting contribution to the lives of not only prairie farm women but all Canadians. Canada recently officially designated Violet McNaughton a "person of national historic significance" because of her lifelong commitment to farmers', citizens', and women's rights.

■ *Violet McNaughton was an eloquent spokesperson for women's rights for more than half a century.*

ment a few months later when William L. Mackenzie King and his Liberal Party trounced Bennett in a national election.

The Rise of the Co-operative Commonwealth Federation

The failure of both the federal and the provincial governments to adequately respond to the poverty and despair of the Dirty Thirties led to notable political developments in Saskatchewan and other western provinces. In 1932 a coalition of western farmers, workers, and progressives met in Calgary to form a new political party. The Co-operative Commonwealth Federation (CCF) most clearly stated its political beliefs the following year at its convention in Regina, where it adopted what came to be known as the Regina Manifesto. Radical by the standards of that time, the manifesto supported nationalizing key

industries in order to create a mixed economy (part private enterprise and part government supported). The manifesto also defended the need for social programs that can supply a safety net for disadvantaged citizens. This included reforms, such as unemployment insurance and workers' compensation, that many Western democracies eventually adopted.

During the 1930s and early 1940s the populist CCF party backed a number of successful candidates in Saskatchewan and other, mostly western, provinces. It also elected a few members to the federal legislature. It was most successful, however, in Saskatchewan, where in 1944 its provincial leader, Scottish-born Thomas Douglas, was elected premier. A former printer and preacher, Douglas was the first socialist premier of a province in Canadian history. Over his seventeen-year reign, he solidified Saskatchewan's reputation for progressive social programs by pioneering programs ranging from old-age pensions to public health care.

■ *During his long political career Tommy Douglas won over many Saskatchewan voters with entertaining and humorous stump speeches.*

A Pioneer in Public Health Care

After Douglas's election, his CCF government wasted little time in passing laws to support health, education, and welfare. For example, the Health Care Insurance Act was essentially, notes health writer Marlene Piturro, "tax-financed hospitalization administered by a quasi-governmental agency."[19] The system was gradually expanded and more funds were devoted to health care, though not without overcoming strong opposition—including protest strikes—from the province's doctors. At its height in the 1970s Saskatchewan's program included not only hospitalization, office visits, and routine medical procedures, but also prescription drugs, chiropractic care, even childhood orthodontics. High costs have since caused the benefits to be trimmed back.

The Canadian government has in recent years copied and adapted this public health model. In 1968 a federal law stipulated that the provinces and federal government evenly split the cost of a comprehensive and accessible package of medical services. Canada's current system of public health care took shape in 1984 with the passage of the Canada Health Act. Although the federal system has come under fire in recent years because of concerns related to quality, funding, and the spiraling cost of prescription drugs, the concept of publicly administered, universal health care that originated in Saskatchewan is still respected by the vast majority of Canadians.

A Prime Minister from Saskatchewan

Thomas Douglas went on to national leadership of the New Democratic Party (NDP), which evolved out of the CCF in 1961. After Douglas's death at age eighty-one in 1986, he was memorialized in the names of streets, schools, buildings, and parks throughout Saskatchewan. One of the most notable memorials is the Douglas Provincial Park, with its twelve miles (twenty kilometers) of white sand beaches along the southeast coast of Lake Diefenbaker. This reservoir itself is named after a prominent Saskatchewan politician who was one of Douglas's chief rivals on the national scene from the 1950s through the 1970s.

John Diefenbaker managed to extend Saskatchewan's commitment to social welfare to the national scene by being elected the country's prime minister in 1957. His political vision for Canada—a mix of concern for the poor with plans for economic development—was in tune with the name of his party, the Progressive Conservatives. Diefenbaker promoted wheat sales to China, a boon for Saskatchewan's farmers. He also was behind the expansion of First Nations' rights, with Canada extending the right to vote to all aboriginals. Diefenbaker promoted the "Canadian Bill of Rights," led an anti-apartheid campaign against South Africa, and appointed the first woman cabinet minister. He lost a close election for a second term in 1963, in part because of his adamant opposition to stationing American nuclear weapons on Canadian soil.

After Douglas and Diefenbaker, Saskatchewan had to wait until the 1990s before it once again found a leader of national

■ "Dief the Chief"

John Diefenbaker was born to parents of German and Scottish heritage in Ontario in 1895. His family moved to a Fort Carlton homestead in 1903, two years before the establishment of Saskatchewan as a province, and then to Saskatoon in 1910. As a youngster, Diefenbaker was inspired by a book about Laurier, who served as prime minister from 1896 to 1911, and decided to become a political leader. Diefenbaker received bachelor's and master's degrees from the University of Saskatchewan and then served briefly in the army. He obtained a law degree and opened a practice as a criminal lawyer in 1920 in Prince Albert.

An effective public speaker and a natural for politics, he nevertheless lost his first five attempts at election to provincial and federal positions. In the 1930s he became head of the Saskatchewan Conservative Party and was finally elected a Member of Parliament in 1940. He effectively challenged the ruling Liberal Party, which had been in power since Bennett's loss in 1935, and thereby earned the respect of his colleagues in the national Progressive Conservative Party.

Finally gaining the leadership of his party in 1956, Diefenbaker ran a shrewd campaign to win the election as prime minister the following year. "Part circus barker, part vaudeville actor, Diefenbaker's theatrical delivery entertained Canadians," noted Craig I.W. Marlatt, "and his appeal to the farmer, store-owner and factory-worker won their hearts and their votes. He became 'Dief, the Chief.'"

Diefenbaker led his country for six years and stayed politically active on the national scene for the next two decades. After his death in Ottawa in 1979, the final train journey to his burial site in Saskatoon was an emotional one for the entire nation. As Prime Minister Joe Clark said in his eulogy to Diefenbaker, "It is easier to change laws than to change lives. John Diefenbaker changed both. His Bill of Rights, his social programs, his resource and regional development policies, changed permanently the laws of Canada. But, more fundamental than that, he changed our vision of our country. He opened the nation to itself, and let us see our possibilities."

■ *On the campaign trail in Ontario in 1963, John Diefenbaker meets with Iroquois chief Split Water.*

stature who could sustain the province's long-standing commitment to social welfare.

A Brush with Bankruptcy

In 1982 the people of Saskatchewan, apparently tired of almost half a century of rule by either the Liberal Party or the CCF/NDP, elected a Progressive Conservative Party (PCP) government under the leadership of Premier D. Grant Devine. The new government attempted to ride the momentum of the 1970s resource boom by instituting a number of dramatic new policies. To attract new businesses to Saskatchewan, it reduced personal and corporate tax rates, lowered the royalty rate companies had to pay the province for the extraction of nonrenewable resources, and increased subsidies for private businesses. Such policies helped the province attract new businesses and create jobs. But the reduced government revenue caused the province to run up a huge $15 billion debt, which was the largest per-capita debt among any of the provinces.

The looming financial crisis led to the Progressive Conservative's defeat by the NDP in 1991 and the election of politically savvy lawyer Roy Romanow as premier. During his three terms Romanow managed to reduce the debt and achieve balanced annual budgets without drastically raising taxes or sacrificing social programs. "With the possible exception of [Alberta's] Ralph Kline, Romanow was the most successful provincial politician of the 1990s," according to *Pundit Magazine*. "Even those who hold vastly different views from the long-time New Democrat," a review noted, "acknowledge that his problem-solving abilities are a tremendous asset, and he proved his ability to overcome steep challenges early in his first mandate, when he began the arduous task of getting the finances of his nearly bankrupt province back in order."[20]

Urban Versus Rural

During the early 1990s, more than a dozen former legislators from Devine's government were convicted of fraud as a result of various scandals during their time in office. Saskatchewan's Progressive Conservative Party never fully recovered. By the mid-1990s the PCP had withdrawn from future elections and effectively left the ruling New Democrats without opposition.

The political void left by the self-destruction of Saskatchewan's Progressive Conservative Party in the early 1990s was short-lived. In 1997 eight members of the provincial legislature united to form the Saskatchewan Party (SP). The new party adopted a platform similar to that of the Republican Party in the United States, pledging to cut taxes and reduce government spending, support a free-market economy to create more private-sector jobs, crack down on crime, and replace welfare with workfare. Led by the feisty farmer and politician Elwin Hermanson, the Saskatchewan Party quickly became the only viable opposition party to the NDP.

Despite NDP efforts to portray the Saskatchewan Party as out of touch with the province's longtime commitment to ethnic diversity and social justice, the SP almost won the 1999 general election. A strong showing among farmers and rural voters allowed it to capture more of the popular vote than the NDP and just short of half of the fifty-eight seats in the provincial legislature. The NDP, its support now mainly the urbanites of Regina and Saskatoon, managed to stay in power only by forming a coalition government with the small Liberal Party.

The current urban-rural split in Saskatchewan politics reflects what may well be a growing disparity between the daily lives of those who live in the province's two major metropolitan areas, Regina and Saskatoon, and those who have remained in the struggling prairie towns.

Daily Life

I n many ways everyday life in Saskatchewan reflects trends common throughout Canada. The province has a reputation as a farm belt, yet 40 percent of Saskatchewan residents live in either the Saskatoon or the Regina metropolitan areas and 25 percent of the province's workers are government employees. Even though no other cities in Saskatchewan approach the dynamic duo in size or influence (the next-largest city, Prince Albert, has a total population only one-fifth the size of either), more than two-thirds of the province's residents are now considered urban. As is true in most of the rest of Canada, this is a much higher figure than forty years ago. A closer look at Saskatchewan's two truly urban areas provides a clearer portrait of the province and its people.

Regina: Queen City of the Prairies

Few cities in the world have been founded on sites that have Regina's paucity of natural features. After all, the most prominent aspect of the site, located on the banks of a muddy stream, was a pile of bones. Regina is not on the edge of a parkland belt, like Saskatoon, but rather smack in the middle of flat, virtually treeless prairie. Yet the people of Regina have created a bustling, tree-lined, and attractive city on this unpromising location. Regina appears almost as an oasis in the midst of wheat fields, with its many parks and a large, island-dotted lake. And it is all human-made over little more than a century.

Regina's founders early on realized that the city would need shade. The municipality started to plant trees and has not stopped. The compact city now boasts more than 350,000 native and exotic trees lining streets and bunched in parks. Trees now provide not only beauty and shade but clues to Regina's history, as a pair of travel writers noted more than thirty years ago.

Reginans judge the age of various sections of town by the height of the trees. In the beginning "there wasn't a sprig anywhere around," reported one old-timer. Over the last fifty years thousands of trees have been imported, painstakingly watered in summer and protected from the prairie blizzards in the winter. Beyond the downtown areas, where the firs and maples may rise above the gabled houses, trees are no more than roof high, and in the suburbs, where the streets run straight into the open prairie, homes stand out in their fresh pastel paint because the trees are still only striplings.[21]

The muddy Wascana Creek that served as the site for butchering buffalo long ago is now a tree-lined park meandering through Regina, its banks crowded with stands of cattail, bulrush, and sedges. During the city's infancy officials dammed the creek on the outskirts of the town to create the 300-acre (121-hectare) Wascana Lake. The lake in turn has become the centerpiece of Wascana Centre, the largest urban park in North America. The Centre is eight times larger than Regina's downtown core and roughly three times the size of New York's Central Park.

■ Regina's grandly conceived Legislative Building on Wascana Lake is a functioning government center as well as a tourist attraction.

The Centre is mostly landscaped hills and meadows but it is also the site of various buildings, most prominently the architecturally impressive Legislative Building that was completed in 1919 at considerable cost. With its columned beaux-arts façade, stately dome, relief-sculpted pediment, formal gardens, and thirty-four types of marble used in the interior,

■ An Oasis Within the Oasis

The people of Regina love the Wascana Centre, a huge oasis within the city. Especially during the summer they flock to the park's playgrounds, fountains (including one that once stood in London's Trafalgar Square), paved bike routes, and sports fields. The bird sanctuary is a popular viewing site for mallards, marsh wrens, killdeer, and blue-winged teals. The picnic areas and flower beds feature a variety of exotic and native plants, from snowberry to Lewis flax. The lake, which in the 1930s was drained to deepen and enlarge it, has a busy marina and a ferry for transport to Willow Island. The Albert Street Memorial Bridge, noted for its hundreds of colored columns, has been described by "Ripley's Believe It or Not" as "the longest bridge across the smallest body of water in the world."

The Wascana Centre is also home to the campus of the University of Regina, a museum and performing arts complex, and a science center. Another attraction is the restored boyhood home of the late Canadian prime minister John Diefenbaker, moved here from its original location near Borden, west of Saskatoon.

it has been compared in grandeur to France's Palace of Versailles. The building is surrounded by 165 acres (67 hectares) of landscaped gardens.

In addition to being the governmental capital, Regina has become a viable commercial and administrative center. Its banks, offices, and transportation facilities serve the industries that deliver grain, oil, and potash to Canada and the world. The downtown has a lively mix of art galleries and theaters, although Regina is generally conceded to yield to Saskatoon as cultural capital of the province. At some point in the mid-1980s, Regina also fell behind Saskatoon in population. Much like the bigger cities of Edmonton and Calgary in neighboring Alberta, there is a history of friendly rivalry between the two principal Saskatchewan cities that is played out in corporate offices as well as in the hockey rinks and on the football fields.

Saskatoon: City of Sun and Bridges

Centrally located within the southern half of the province, Saskatoon has developed into a vibrant city of broad streets, low-rise buildings, and winding parks. Its population of approximately two hundred thousand makes it the largest metropolitan area in the province. The area, if not the exact site of the city, has been inhabited continuously by First Nations peoples since perhaps 5000 B.C. In the mid–nineteenth century the local Cree referred to the stopover site as "mis-sask-quah-toomina," *misaskwatomin* referring apparently to a local tree that supplied the Indians with berries as well as supple wood to make bows. In 1882 John Lake scouted the site for the Ontario-based Temperance Colonization Society, and three dozen settlers from the society arrived the following year. Lake apparently respected native rights enough to at least anglicize their name and he dubbed the new settlement Saskatoon.

The no-alcohol policy of the temperance society founders did not last long as the new settlement attracted merchants and others willing to serve the growing agricultural economy. The first railway, a short line linking Saskatoon to Regina, arrived in 1890. By 1909, when Saskatoon was chosen as the site for the province's university, the city's future as a business, distribution, railway, and education center was assured. The booming wheat business caused Saskatoon's population to reach almost thirty thousand in 1912, although growth slowed in the hard times of the World War I and Great Depression years.

Today the influence of the University of Saskatchewan, located on a tree-lined campus across the South Saskatchewan River from the heart of the city, has helped Saskatoon to become a cultural center, with plenty of museums, art galleries, craft shops, a zoo, and other attractions. The university is the city's leading employer and many of its graduates stay on to work in the adjacent research park, now bustling with high-

■ *Saskatoon's Delta Bessborough Hotel, built in 1928 and renovated in 2000, is a major landmark on the banks of the South Saskatchewan River.*

tech, biotechnology, and communications companies. Saskatoon remains a center for farming, food processing, and meatpacking. In recent years the city has added many businesses that serve the mining and transportation industries. The clean air from Saskatoon's lack of pollution-heavy industry and its many hours of annual sunshine contribute to the city's reputation for livability.

Like the Wascana Centre in Regina, the South Saskatchewan River is a major presence in Saskatoon. The winding river and adjacent parkland bisect the city and provide popular recreational sites and trails for joggers, bicyclists, and cross-country skiers. The seven bridges crossing the South Saskatchewan within city limits led to Saskatoon being dubbed the "City of Bridges." The river, along with the Trans Canada Yellowhead Highway and the Grand Trunk Pacific Railway, also connects Saskatoon with the surrounding farmland.

Farming as a Family Endeavor

Even as grain farms grow in size in Saskatchewan, most are still family owned and operated. Farm houses are often modest considering that the average farm, now two square miles (five square kilometers) in size, can be worth half a million dollars where land sells for $60,000 per quarter square mile. Such "paper values" can be misleading, however, given the difficulties prairie farmers have faced in recent years. "When I began farming," prairie grain farmer George E. Hickie noted recently, "out of each growing dollar I was able to retain 48 cents for personal use. Today, only six cents is left for myself and my family."[22]

Financial difficulties mean that many farmers still rely on labor from the whole family to succeed. Teens may quit school at sixteen to help their parents farm. Even preteens are expected to chip in by tending to the family garden, feeding livestock, or driving a tractor or all-terrain vehicle. Family labor may be complemented during the busiest times, such as harvest, by hired help, although a strong tradition of help-thy-neighbor exists in Saskatchewan. "Neighbors usually help one another out—you don't worry about getting paid. If you help your neighbor one year, you're almost guaranteed that, if there is some way he can help, he'll give you a hand the next,"[23] says second-generation farmer Don Bashutski of Lestock, near Yorkton.

Life on many of the grain farms of southern and central Saskatchewan is still dictated by the seasons. Seeding of wheat and other crops begins in late April and continues until early June. During the growing season farmers may add fertilizer and spray herbicides and pesticides to control weeds and kill unwelcome insects such as grasshoppers. July and August is the time to cut hay, which is needed to feed the cattle during the winter. Cows need little tending after they are put out to pasture during the summer but have to be watched closely, fed, and watered during the freezing winters.

Harvesting grain crops during September and October is accomplished using a swather, which cuts the stalks and drops them on the ground in windrows so the grain can dry. After a few days or weeks, depending on the weather, grain farmers finish the harvest by traversing their fields with a combine that separates the grain from the chaff. When the weather or other factors hinder harvest, farmers may have to work twenty-hour days. Even with the northern sun extending summer daylight beyond 9:00 P.M., farmers often rely on floodlights and machinery headlights to work past midnight.

■ *Farmers harvest a grain field in Riceton, a small town south of Regina.*

Life on the Reserves

Like its farms and cities, most of Saskatchewan's seventy First Nations reserves are scattered throughout the southern half of the province. (The spacing of the reserves is no accident:

Officials set them up that way to discourage tribes from forming antigovernment alliances.) Reserves are typically small to moderately sized, in total taking up less than 2 percent of Saskatchewan's land base. Of the estimated one hundred thousand First Nations people residing in Saskatchewan (up from a mere forty thousand in the province three decades earlier), approximately half live on one of the reserves. Many of the remaining live in the Saskatoon or Regina metropolitan areas.

A few of the Indian reserves hold only a smattering of residents, as is the case with the Ocean Man Reserve located near Moose Mountain Provincial Park in the southeast corner of the province. It holds only fifty-some Assiniboines, though the band has more than three hundred registered members. Other reserves hold thousands of residents and operate much like small towns. For example, the Mistawasis Indian Reserve west of Prince Albert has almost two thousand registered members and operates its own administration center and community health facility. (The band, descended from Woodland Cree, is named after its first chief, Mistawasis, who signed Treaty 6 in 1876.) The Mistawasis First Nations' school educates children through grade nine (high school students are bused to nearby Leask). The Sakihtowin (Cree for "let us love one another") Daycare Center, which opened in 1997, can take care of a dozen children.

Mistawasis's current chief, Melvin Watson, is a former farmer and carpenter who with his wife owns and operates a store that sells groceries, gas, and videos. Other community

■ *Ranchers herd cattle in Bengough, "Gateway to the Big Muddy."*

■ Vanishing Wooden Skyscrapers

One of the most distinctive symbols of Saskatchewan is found in the province's once-widespread collection of small-town grain elevators. The province's earliest "crib style" wooden grain elevators were built in the 1880s. During the wheat boom years almost every town boasted its own elevator; an estimated three thousand existed by the late 1930s. The boxy wooden elevators are simple but handsome buildings, some soaring more than eighty feet (twenty-five meters) high. They stand proud on the prairie even as a new generation of more massive cylindrical concrete elevators replaces them.

Wooden grain elevators' stark vertical architecture is directly tied to their main function as transfer stations. A farmer would drive his grain-laden truck into the elevator building. The truck would be weighed and then the grain dumped through a hatch in the floor into a temporary storage pit. The elevator operator would take some grain samples for testing; factors such as moisture content and grade would determine to which of the elevator's many bins the grain would be sent. The operator could move the grain via a complex system of scoops, buckets, conveyor belts, distributors, and spouts. The empty truck would then be weighed to determine how much grain had been offloaded. The farmer would be paid and the grain stored until sold and transferred to a truck or a railcar (most elevators are located on rail lines). Saskatchewan grain would be shipped to a mill for processing or to ports for export.

As few as three hundred of the classic wooden grain elevators still exist in Saskatchewan. One has recently been converted into a wheat museum (the Hepburn Museum of Wheat, located in a Saskatoon-area elevator built in 1927). Some burned down but many have been demolished over the past decade in favor of the more mechanized "inland terminals." A single one of these modern facilities can replace a dozen of the wooden buildings, although the improved efficiency—the ability to handle fifty grain cars at a time rather than the five or ten of the wooden elevators—is often accompanied by a social cost. A small town's loss of its elevator means not only fewer jobs and reduced tax dollars, but also the loss of a building that acted as a focal point of the community as well as a draw for commercial activity in the rest of town.

■ *Wooden grain elevators line the tracks in Morse, a farming community between Moose Jaw and Swift Current.*

businesses include a cattle operation, a building-moving company, a casket design and construction company, and a cultural village/ecotourism project. Typically the native businesses market to everyone, but much of their clientele are First Nations people. Even on such reserves with viable businesses, many natives continue nevertheless to live in relative poverty. Reserve Indians often suffer from higher than average rates of unemployment, suicide, alcoholism, and infant mortality.

■ The New Urban Reserves

Some of the most unusual reserves in Saskatchewan as well as all of Canada are located within the province's towns and cities. Natives have increasingly bought up land to build urban reserves since the first one, the Opawakoscikan Reserve, was established by the Peter Ballantyne (Cree) Band in Prince Albert in the early 1980s.

The new urban reserves got a boost in 1992 when more than two dozen First Nations signed the Treaty Land Entitlement Agreement (TLEA) with the province and the federal government. The TLEA set aside $500 million over a twelve-year period to allow tribes to purchase land, whether it is put on the market by private or public sources. After the purchase of the land, tribes can apply to the federal government to have it designated as a reserve. Many tribes have taken the opportunity to purchase land within cities, with an eye on developing the land for commercial purposes, including gambling casinos, office buildings, strip malls, and housing. Such businesses can provide much-needed economic benefits for the many Indians who live off-reserve. Urban reserves have been established in Saskatoon as well as in smaller cities and towns including Yorkton, Meadow Lake, and Fort Qu'Appelle.

New urban reserves can be established only after natives and government officials negotiate a variety of sometimes-thorny issues. Taxation is a major concern because only tribes are allowed to collect taxes on reserves. City managers fear the loss of their tax base if tribes control larger and larger plots of urban land. City services are another major issue. Indians realize that, because they are not paying taxes, they need to negotiate for the delivery of services such as water and sewer. In most instances Indian groups and city or provincial officials have achieved successful compromise agreements. For example, after the establishment of Saskatchewan's twentieth urban reserve in North Battleford in early 2002, Wayne Ray, the city's mayor, called the agreement with the Mosquito/Grizzly Bear's Head/Lean Man First Nation, an Assiniboine band, "a win-win situation for the citizens of the city and the First Nations" that would create new jobs and expand economic opportunities.

Diverse Educational Opportunities

Canadian law requires that Saskatchewan provide a free public education to all students in kindergarten through high school. The province stipulates school attendance from the day a child turns seven until the day he or she turns sixteen. Approximately 1 percent of the province's two hundred thousand kindergarten-through grade-twelve students are homeschooled; another 2 percent attend private (independent) schools. Thus the vast majority of Saskatchewan students go to publicly funded schools, including religious schools. (Saskatchewan is one of five provinces that provides funding for religious schools.) The province provides about 40 percent of K–12 school funding while the rest comes from locally generated property taxes.

Saskatchewan's 850 or so schools are organized into more than fifty school divisions, including eight Roman Catholic divisions and one French-speaking "scholaire Francophone" division. For example, Saskatoon has both a public school division (with forty-four elementary schools and eight high schools serving approximately twenty-two thousand students) and a Catholic division (with thirty-four elementary schools and five high schools serving more than fifteen thousand students). Such large divisions each employ more than one thousand people in their teaching, service, and support staffs and are overseen by separate, elected boards of education. The boards do not control teacher salaries, which are set

■ Raising the Education Bar

Saskatchewan is seeking to increase its emphasis on education because it currently ranks somewhat low by Canadian standards in average level of education attained by its residents. A 1996 survey found that the province ranked tenth among the twelve provinces and territories in the percentage of high school graduates among residents age twenty-five to twenty-nine. Saskatchewan's figure of 63 percent was ahead of only Newfoundland and Northwest Territories and was well below the national average of 72 percent. Another survey the same year ranked Saskatchewan ninth for average years of schooling, at 11.8 years. (The Canadian average was 12.3 years.) Saskatchewan is also below the Canadian average for percentage of post-secondary graduates among twenty-five- to fifty-four-year-olds. Such low figures present a challenge for the province in the coming years, as companies seek to locate in areas where they can hire workers with high educational levels.

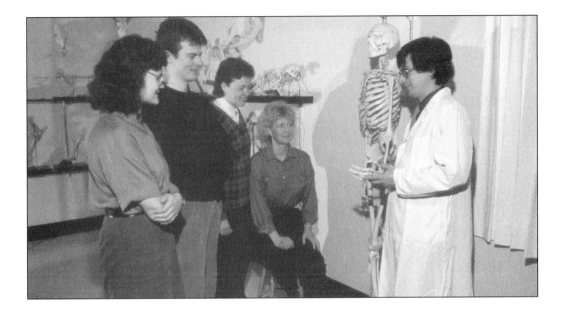

in negotiations between the teachers and the province, but they do hire teachers and principals and work within provincial standards to shape the curriculum. The boards in turn take advice and direction from local school committees made up of parents and community members.

The province's only two universities are located in its major cities. The University of Saskatchewan in Saskatoon was established in 1909, much to the dismay of the people of Regina. The capital city was awarded only a campus of the provincial university. This campus, however, was made a separate university, the University of Regina, in 1974. The University of Saskatchewan is best known for its departments of agriculture, computer systems, and life sciences. It is the only university in Canada to offer the full range of degrees in medicine, nursing, veterinary, dentistry, and pharmacy. The University of Regina, in addition to renowned departments of fine arts, journalism, and aboriginal studies, has the only First Nations–run university-affiliated college in Canada, the Saskatchewan Indian Federated College. Founded in 1976 and currently teaching some two thousand students, the college has adjunct campuses in Saskatoon and Prince Albert and arranges for courses to be taught in more remote parts of the province. Students in Saskatchewan can also pursue postsecondary education at the four-campus Saskatchewan Institute of Applied Science and Technology, nine community colleges, and more than fifty vocational schools and career colleges.

■ *An instructor uses a skeleton to help teach an anatomy class at the University of Saskatchewan.*

A Commitment to Wellness and Preventive Care

After taking a pioneering role in the development of public health care in the mid–twentieth century, Saskatchewan remains strongly committed to the concept today. Since the early 1980s Canada has offered a nationalized health care program that is jointly funded by the federal and provincial governments although administered solely by provincial governments. In 2002 health care accounted for about $2.2 billion—almost 40 percent—of Saskatchewan's overall budget. All provincial residents, regardless of income or employment status, have their basic health care needs, including hospitalization, covered.

Saskatchewan has not been immune, however, to some of the same health care-related problems that other provinces have experienced in the past decade. Many of these problems can be traced to reduced national funding at a time when federal requirements have increased and costs for drugs and medical services have skyrocketed. Saskatchewan thus has experienced long wait times for certain types of procedures and a shortage of key health care providers, especially in rural areas. Saskatchewan also faces the challenge of providing care to the people who live in small towns that may be quite distant from clinics and hospitals.

Saskatchewan officials have resisted urging the types of radical reforms bandied about in other provinces. In Alberta, for example, political leaders have recently been calling for greater privatization of the system and a return to fee-for-service billing. Rather than abandoning the long commitment in Saskatchewan to public health, the ruling New Democratic Party has responded to the growing health care crisis by promoting a new "wellness model" for health care. This would increase the emphasis on preventive care by offering services such as a twenty-four-hour call-in advice line. A recent government action plan recommended that Saskatchewan keep open all of its hospitals and institute a province-wide surgical waiting list to reduce wait times and make them more fair.

Football and Hockey Rule

Although work, education, and health care are important everyday issues in the province, throughout Saskatchewan people also find the time for a variety of recreational activities, from birdwatching to hang-gliding. Wilderness canoeing is a prime outdoor activity in Saskatchewan, with its one hundred thousand freshwater lakes and numerous rivers in the northern two-thirds of the province. In the winter many active people turn to skiing, skating, curling, and snowmobiling. Of course, team sports are also a year-round activity in Saskatchewan, both for participating and spectating.

The most popular professional sports team in the province is the Saskatchewan Roughriders of the Canadian Football League. The Roughriders play their games in the twenty-eight-thousand-seat Taylor Field in Regina. The team has not been overly successful on the field—it has won the league championship only twice, most recently in 1989—but it still attracts fan interest from around the province, especially for meetings with close rivals Winnipeg and Calgary. Saskatchewan's entries in the Prairie Football Conference of the Canadian Junior Football League, the Regina Rams and the Saskatoon Hilltops, have a long history of spirited rivalry.

The province's two main cities are not large enough to support an entry in North America's professional National Hockey League (NHL). Ice hockey remains, however, a major sport for both spectators and participants. Saskatchewan has thirteen "Junior-A" (top minor league) hockey teams that play sixty-plus game schedules, with the hard-fought contests often drawing one thousand or more in attendance. Some of these players go on to NHL stardom—goalie Curtis Joseph,

■ *Saskatchewan curlers compete on ice sheets in an indoor curling rink.*

■ *The Regina Rams have been a dominant force in amateur football in Canada since their formation in the mid-1950s.*

for example, played for the Notre Dame Hounds of Wilcox. Saskatchewan also has hundreds of local amateur leagues for boys and girls, from infants to seniors.

In addition to hockey, Saskatchewan's residents are particularly avid golfers. With more than 250 courses serving its population of slightly less than a million, Saskatchewan has more golf courses per capita than any other place in the world. Some of the province's oldest golf courses have unusual flat greens made of sand, since the arid climate makes it difficult to keep grass lush and green. The sand greens are a fairly dense mixture of sand and oil (nowadays vegetable rather than petroleum). Golfers use a special rakelike roller to smooth their footsteps after putting, leaving a flat surface for golfers who follow.

A Lively Cultural Scene

It is not surprising that the province offers a host of hard-to-match recreational opportunities, given the many interesting natural locales, from lakeside beaches to mountain streams. Perhaps more surprising is that Saskatchewan also enjoys a lively cultural scene complete with talented artists, innovative filmmakers, and popular musicians. Saskatchewan officials have long recognized the arts as a provincial asset worth cherishing—and funding.

Arts and Culture

S
askatchewan was a pioneer not only in establishing social welfare programs but also in promoting the arts. In 1948 the provincial government formed the Saskatchewan Arts Board, the first governmental body of its kind in North America. Its mandate was to promote small theater groups, struggling writers and painters, and independent galleries. The Regina-based board has since served as a model for similar agencies created in other provinces as well as American states. It remains a vital source of arts funding in the province today, operating on an annual budget of approximately $4 million—90 percent of which comes from the provincial government. The board offers scholarships and grants as well as various programs and services to artists, cultural workers, and groups. It also buys and preserves art created by provincial residents and now has a more extensive collection of Saskatchewan art than any gallery or museum.

Official support for the arts only partly explains why Saskatchewan has such a lively cultural scene. The large native population in the province continues unique artistic and cultural traditions. Saskatchewan's diverse ethnic cultures and its pioneer heritage provide inspiration for a fascinating array of festivals, rodeos, museums, and other events and institutions.

Modern Native Art

Cree, Assiniboine, Dene, and other aboriginal artists are today creating artwork in dozens of media. These include not only paintings, drawings, woodwork, and jewelry but also decorated birchbark and red willow baskets; colorful blankets and star quilts; intricately beaded moccasins; handcarved bows and arrows; elaborate dreamcatchers (embroidered hoops hung near the sleeping place to catch the good dreams

■ Cree Artist Allen Sapp

Saskatchewan's most successful and celebrated native artist may be Allen Sapp, an elderly Cree painter whose pictures evoke early–twentieth century tribal life. "I can't write a story or tell one in the white man's language," Sapp notes on his website, "so I tell what I want to say with my paintings. . . . I put it down so it doesn't get lost and people will be able to see and remember." Over the past three decades Sapp's work has toured throughout Canada and the United States, he has been elected to the Royal Canadian Academy of Arts, and he has had numerous books and documentaries devoted to his life and art.

Sapp was born on the Red Pheasant Indian Reserve south of North Battleford in 1928 into a Cree family that grew to include seven siblings. The Sapps struggled through the Dirty Thirties, as did most Indians. During childhood Allen had a near-fatal bout with spinal meningitis that kept him bedridden for months, and by the time he was seventeen four of his brothers and sisters had died from tuberculosis and other causes.

Sapp developed a love of painting as a young child. He was a keen observer and possessed an almost photographic memory—his grandmother gave him the Cree name *Kiskayetum,* "he perceives it." For much of his youth and well into his adulthood, however, his paintings were more or less divorced from his experience as a Cree. By the early 1960s he had a wife and a son and was living in a humble house in North Battleford, trying to make it as an artist by painting nature scenes that he hoped would appeal to whites.

In 1966 he met Allan Gonor, a doctor at the North Battleford Medical Clinic and a discerning art collector. Gonor recognized Sapp's innate talent

and dispel the bad); and striking leatherwork (pictures carved on leather and then dyed).

The nonprofit, Saskatoon-based Saskatchewan Indian Cultural Centre (SICC) is in the process of establishing a native-controlled and -operated museum, the First Nations Keeping House, to house some of this original art. The museum will help to broaden the cultural awareness of First Nations people and raise funds for the center's efforts to support native education, art, and cultures. The SICC is currently operating the Aboriginal Arts Gallery Saskatchewan, an online version of the Keeping House. The gallery has photos and descriptions of the work of almost two hundred native artists, and some of the items are available for purchase.

and encouraged the artist to paint from his experience as a Cree. This proved to be a turning point in Sapp's life. He gradually rediscovered his native identity, let his crewcut grow to braids, and began to depict in his oil and acrylic paintings scenes he could still vividly recall from his childhood experience on the Indian reserve. Some of his most touching paintings, of a horse-drawn sled passing by or of a group of children on a frozen pond, seem to be from the point of view of a child perched in a tree. His first major exhibition of these new paintings, at the Mendel Art Gallery in Saskatoon in 1968, was a public sensation. He sold almost all of the sixty-one paintings on exhibit by the first night and has hardly been able to keep up with the demand for his paintings since then.

In 1989, shortly after the death of Gonor, who had become Sapp's good friend and patron, Sapp opened the Allen Sapp Gallery in North Battleford. The Sapp paintings donated by Gonor's wife are a major attraction, though the permanent collection now includes the work of many other native artists.

■ *"Baby Was Crying" typifies Sapp's sensitive portrayal of traditional Cree life.*

Many of Saskatchewan's talented native artists are not formally trained professionals but rather gifted amateurs who nevertheless are accomplished in their field of creative activity. For example, Celine Matchee, an elderly member of the (Cree) Flying Dust First Nation, does enchanting and original dreamcatchers, floral arrangements, and ornamental wreaths. She also teaches traditional dancing and drives a school bus on her reserve.

On the other hand, a number of the province's native artists have become nationally and even internationally recognized for their work. Besides the Cree painter Allen Sapp there is portrait artist Robert Bellegarde, who is from the Little Black Bear Reserve near Balcarres; Ruth Cuthand, a Plains

Cree born in Prince Albert who is best known for her circa-nineteenth-century Ghost Dance shirts; and abstract painter and sculptor Calvin Sand, originally from Mistawasis First Nation. Also noteworthy is Edward Poitras, a Métis artist born in Regina who in 1995 became the first aboriginal artist to represent Canada at the prestigious Venice Biennale.

Film and Video

Native as well as nonnative residents of Saskatchewan are also engaged in artistic endeavors that involve the latest high-tech gear, from digital video to mixed media. The film industry in particular has been one of the most visible recipients of provincial support for the arts. Revenue from the production of films in the province increased approximately ten fold during the 1990s, to a $60 million-per-year business employing some seven hundred residents by 2001. Saskatchewan has more than forty motion picture and video production and postproduction companies, among them the prominent Regina-based companies Minds Eye Pictures and Partners in Motion. The former is western Canada's largest film and television production company while a documentary (13 Seconds: The Kent State Shootings) shot by the latter won the first Emmy for a Saskatchewan film company in 2001.

In the fall of 2002 the province opened a major new film and video production and training facility in Regina. The state-of-the-art Canada-Saskatchewan Soundstage was built for $12 million by a partnership of film companies and the city, provincial, and federal governments. It is one of the largest facilities of its kind in western Canada and is expected to attract both Canadian and American companies that want to produce films, television series, animations, and other programming.

Saskatchewan's diverse offering of possible locales and architecture allows filmmakers to shoot everything from modern urban to pioneer western scenes. The nonprofit agency Sask-Film promotes the province as a potential host for film projects and assists with location scouting, permitting, finding crew, and working with support facilities. The province also has an active trade association, the Saskatchewan Motion Picture Association. Established in 1985, it distributes financial support (raised through the provincial lottery) to film and video artists, provides education and production opportunities, holds workshops and cultural events, and publishes monthly and quarterly newsletters that keep members abreast of developments in the Saskatchewan film industry. The association also organizes the biannual NextFest (celebrating video, digital, and mixed media) and the Saskatchewan Film and Video Showcase, as well as other events and festivals in Saskatoon, Yorkton (site of the oldest continuously running short film festival in North America), and elsewhere in the province.

From Rodeos to Jazz Festivals

The lively arts scene in Saskatchewan spills over into an events schedule that peaks during the pleasant summer months. Attractions include everything from Shakespeare revivals to Oktoberfests to jazz festivals. Certainly among the most popular are Saskatchewan's many western-oriented events. For example, Saskatchewan is host to Canada's oldest rodeo, the Wood Mountain Stampede. It has been an annual mid-July event in Wood Mountain, a small village just north of Grasslands National Park, since the early 1890s.

Another popular annual western event is Regina's Buffalo Days, a six-day celebration held in July or August. Residents put on their cowboy hats and western shirts to watch parades, circuses, and concerts and to whoop it up at the rodeo, with such popular events as bull riding, steer wrestling, and barrel racing. In a similar vein, the province's largest annual event is the Saskatoon Exhibition, a week-long August agricultural festival and trade show that includes chuck wagon races, nightly

■ *Regina's three-day Flatland Music Festival has become an annual summer highlight.*

■ Wanuskewin Heritage Park

Located just north of Saskatoon, Wanuskewin Heritage Park is a joint project of local First Nations people, the city of Saskatoon, the provincial and federal governments, and the University of Saskatchewan. The park is a relatively new attraction (established in 1992) that has already become one of the most popular tourist sites in the province. Cree for "seeking peace of mind," Wanuskewin (wah-nus-KAY-win) is an apt name for this oasislike park set on the edge of the prairie. The 300-acre (120-hectare) site includes mixed-grass prairie uplands and a tree-sheltered valley where the Opimihaw Creek runs into the South Saskatchewan River. Trails that wander through the park provide an intimate look at diverse plants, birds, and animals.

The picturesque landscape is enticing but the most remarkable aspect of the park is its ability to foster appreciation of the area's human heritage. Hunter-gatherers lived in the area some six thousand years ago. In more recent times various Northern Plains Indian tribes have sought inspiration, food, and shelter from the land. The Plains Cree are among the last tribes to arrive but the results of archaeological digs suggest that various other tribes camped, hunted, and gathered foods and medicines there, including Lakotah, Dene, and Blackfoot. Because most of the site has never been farmed, many of these digs are well preserved and have yielded an impressive array of native tools and artifacts. Visitors can watch as archaeologists uncover ancient stone cairns, tepee rings, and buffalo jumps (sites where groups of native hunters drove herds of buffalo over cliffs). A must-see is the fifteen-hundred-year-old

concerts and fireworks, a midway and casino, and events such as lumberjack shows and demolition derbies.

Regina celebrates its ethnic diversity, as do a number of other Saskatchewan cities, in an annual cultural festival. Regina's three-days-in-June Mosaic Festival features pavilions throughout the city with Polish, Ukrainian, Métis, First Nations, and other ethnic themes. The pavilions typically offer traditional ethnic foods, live music, and an eclectic entertainment schedule. Visitors can try a *holobsti* (cabbage roll) at the Ukrainian pavilion, have calligraphy done on their skin at the Chinese pavilion, or dance to the rhythmic beat of a steel band at the Caribbean pavilion. A provocative summer attraction in Regina is a regular production of the historic courtroom drama "The Trial of Louis Riel," put on by local actors at the MacKenzie Art Gallery. Typically more than half of the audience is made up of tourists who appreciate the opportunity to gain insight into this still-controversial historic figure.

medicine wheel, a rare alignment of rocks whose exact purpose remains something of a mystery to scientists.

Wanuskewin's boldly designed visitor center, with its four-pointed roof (signifying the four seasons and the four directions) and its earthlike, stone-and-mortar floor, houses an archaeological lab, displays, and sites for hands-on activities. Native guides teach the interested how to bake the traditional unleavened bannock bread, tan a hide, knap a piece of flint to make an arrowhead, or throw a spear using an atlatl. The restaurant in the visitor center offers traditional Indian fare such as buffalo stew, bannock, wild rice, and saskatoon berry pie. Visitors can also watch demonstrations of the Hoop Dance, storytelling, and other traditional performing arts in the site's five-hundred-seat outdoor amphitheater.

■ *Native elders helped to design the striking visitor center at Wanuskewin Heritage Park.*

Saskatoon's many summer attractions include the three-day multicultural Folkfest; a Louis Riel Day with pioneer-era athletic competitions (the hill-scramble leg of a relay race is a favorite among spectators); an exciting Formula One power-boat race on the South Saskatchewan River; and the lively ten-day Saskatchewan Jazz Festival. Saskatoon's International Fringe Festival (with acts ranging from drama to juggling) and its Shakespeare on the Saskatchewan Festival are also prominent summer attractions.

Original Museums and Galleries

Saskatchewan's unique Western Development Museum (WDM) makes up for its drab name with an exciting premise: It re-creates with astonishing reality authentic provincial scenes from bygone time periods. The museum is actually four networked facilities (in Moose Jaw, North Battleford, Yorkton,

■ *The Royal Saskatchewan Museum's five-hundred-year-old Jacobsen Bay Pot is one of the finest examples of First Nations pottery found in the province.*

and Saskatoon), each with separate themes. For example, in North Battleford the Heritage Farm and Village site re-creates the buildings of a small prairie town, including a Wheat Pool grain elevator, co-op store, and churches. Situated throughout the faux-town are restored wagons and early farm machinery, including a huge 1910 Case tractor.

Walk into the WDM indoor boomtown at Saskatoon, notes a travel guide, "and suddenly you're looking down Main St., circa 1910. It looks like a movie set, with stores, workshops, a hotel, a printing shop and other establishments."[24] Volunteers in period costumes offer background information on exhibits ranging from vintage cars and tractors to the 1896 wedding dress of Nellie McClung, probably Canada's most famous writer and women's rights advocate of her era. The WDM branches in Moose Jaw and Yorkton focus respectively on the history of transportation (including a working narrow gauge railway) and the life and times of the province's many immigrant groups, from Ukrainians to Icelanders.

Saskatchewan's museums run the gamut from the traditional (Regina's Royal Saskatchewan Museum, with its displays of Saskatchewan natural history, most notably a half-size Tyrannosaurus rex robot that scares the wits out of some children) to the quirky (the Turner Curling Museum in Weyburn, with its collection of antique curling stones). Depending upon your interests, you can also visit museums devoted to Ukrainian heritage (in Saskatoon), First Nations culture (at Wanuskewin and elsewhere), and railway history (outside Saskatoon). An unusual underground museum can also be found in the colorful town of Moose Jaw.

Loose in Moose Jaw

Even though its population is only about thirty-three thousand, Moose Jaw is Saskatchewan's fourth-largest city and supports its own radio stations, newspaper, and minor league baseball and hockey teams. One of its main tourist attractions is found under its main street, where an intriguing network of basements and tunnels exists that has twice played a prominent role in the city's history.

In 1908 white railway workers in Moose Jaw savagely beat a number of Chinese railway workers, accusing the Chinese of taking jobs away from whites. Although Chinese workers had been instrumental in building the Canadian Pacific Railway in the 1880s, by the beginning of the twentieth century a backlash had set in. "Yellow peril" riots erupted in a number of cities and the Canadian government passed anti-Chinese legislation, including a head tax on new immigrants that had reached $500 by 1904. After the incident in Moose Jaw, according to journalist Dennis Bueckert:

> The Chinese workers literally went underground, digging secret tunnels where they could hide until the situation improved. Evidence suggests the tunnels were used for many

■ *Lifelike figures and authentic products on the shelves help to re-create this scene from a 1910 Saskatchewan boom-town shop at the Western Development Museum in Saskatoon.*

years. The railway workers managed to bring women to live with them and even raised children in rat-infested darkness. Access to the tunnels was gained from the basements of buildings owned by legal Chinese immigrants. The underground residents would do work for above-ground laundries and restaurants and would obtain food and other supplies in payment.[25]

Anti-Chinese sentiments had calmed somewhat by the 1920s, when a second set of characters took over Moose Jaw's tunnels: mob-connected bootleggers. They came to Moose Jaw after the United States prohibited the manufacture, sale, and transportation of liquor in 1919. At the time Canada was also experimenting with prohibition. Canada's liquor ban was less strict than the United States', however, and provinces had more local control. Saskatchewan ended prohibition in 1924; in the United States it lasted until 1933.

Canadian and American prohibition allowed Moose Jaw to become a wild and corrupt place during the 1920s. The police chief and much of the police force were apparently bought off by Chicago mobsters like Al Capone and thus turned a blind eye to bootlegging, gambling, and prostitution in Moose Jaw. Safely across the border from American lawmen, the city became a major supplier and distiller of booze that would be shipped by rail through Minneapolis to Chicago, or driven over the border in the day's most powerful cars. Mobsters used the tunnels as a warehouse for illegal booze and even loaded the liquor directly from the tunnels into a shed on the rail yards.

Located in the heart of Saskatchewan's prairie farmland, a mere forty miles (sixty-four kilometers) west of Regina, Moose Jaw has a number of features beyond its tunnels that attract tourists and Saskatchewan residents alike. A nearby armed forces base, for example, is Canada's busiest airport (by takeoffs and landings) as well as the home of the acrobatic air show Snowbirds jet squadron. Moose Jaw is also within reach of various natural sites that offer a host of recreational opportunities for Saskatchewan's many active residents.

Playlands of the South

One of southern Saskatchewan's most popular outdoor playgrounds is the broad, green, glacially formed Qu'Appelle River valley region just to the east of Regina. The valley has plenty of rich farmland and is also the site of numerous provincial parks and historic sites. Crooked Lake Provincial Park and Echo Valley Provincial Park, for example, offer a wealth of recreational opportunities. Their lakes are popular spots for fishing (including ice fishing during the winter), sailing, and water sports. The Qu'Appelle valley has numerous other sites that attract cross-country skiers, bird watchers, hang gliders, hikers and campers, and golfers. Small children are delighted by the eclectic "world's largest" roadside attractions, such as the twenty-three-foot-(seven-meter) high oil can in Rocanville.

The wide diversity of landscapes in the south also includes the scenic Big Muddy Badlands and the surprising highlands of Cypress Hills Interprovincial Park. One of the best places to experience the prairie is at Grasslands National Park, on the province's border with Montana. The park, established only in 1988, is made up of two plots of land separated by about seventeen miles (twenty-seven kilometers).

■ *Rocanville promotes its image as the "oil can capital of the world" with this outsized oil can.*

■ Touring the Tunnels

For many decades after the 1920s the officials of Moose Jaw downplayed the importance (and even the existence) of the tunnels. Today the history is distant enough to be acknowledged and even celebrated as a unique heritage. Basements and tunnels have been excavated and researched. "The Tunnels of Moose Jaw" have been developed as a popular tourist attraction, complete with animatronic figures—a realistic-looking barkeeper warns onlookers about the corrupt police chief: "Stay out of his way or be ready to pay." Actors and actresses in period costumes and a 1920s-era speakeasy (illegal bar) are now attracting thousands of curious visitors every year.

■ *A prohibition-era agent examines an illegal still used to make alcohol in Moose Jaw's underground tunnels.*

Canada hopes to expand the size of the park (currently 185 square miles, or 478 square kilometers) by buying land as it comes on the market. Visitors come to walk the self-guided nature trails and see a mixed-grass prairie frequented by the relatively rare pronghorn antelope, black-tailed prairie dog, and ferruginous hawk.

Prince Albert National Park

Saskatchewan's other national park, Prince Albert, is located almost smack in the middle of the province, on the southern edge of the boreal forest. It thus has a diverse landscape, including aspen parkland and stands of spruce and pine that host a range of wildlife, including one of the few significant populations of timber wolves left in the world, the second-largest flock of rare white pelicans in Canada, and one of Canada's few small herds (about two hundred animals) of free-ranging plains bison. People visit Prince Albert year-round for hiking, biking, horseback riding, canoeing, fishing,

■ Take a T-Rex Vacation

The small town of Eastend in the far southwestern corner of Saskatchewan was until recently typical of the many small prairie communities struggling to survive on farming or ranching. Over the past decade, however, Eastend has developed an unusual tourist attraction: "Scotty," one of the most complete sets of fossilized Tyrannosaurus rex bones in the world. The bones, displayed in the T-Rex Discovery Center that opened in 2000, were found in the nearby Frenchman River valley. The so-called Frenchman Formation, not far from the last prairie dog towns in Canada, is a dinosaur-hunter's paradise. It is chock-full of fossils, including the recently found first-of-a-kind fossilized T-rex dung, from the era just prior to the dinosaurs' extinction, circa 65 million years ago.

The area has attracted the attention of scientists only since the mid-1970s and fossil-hunters say that new finds are expected. Almost a decade after the first of Scotty's bones was discovered in 1994, researchers are still uncovering parts of the extinct dinosaur. In 2001 paleontologists discovered a shoulder bone and two leg bones that belong to Scotty. Preserving and reconstructing Scotty, one of only a dozen such T-rex fossils in the world, is expected to take years. When completed Scotty will stand sixteen feet (five meters) high and stretch forty-five feet (fourteen meters) in length.

Visitors to the center's fossil research station who are not content to merely watch paleontologists at work in a laboratory can sign up for fieldwork. Experienced fossil hunters lead small groups to sites where they can engage in a day- or week-long "dinosaur-dig vacation." "Physically, you'd do the same thing a paleontologist would do when he [or she] finds a site," Bruce Lewis told Virtual Saskatchewan's Dave Yanko.

■ *Staff members of the Royal Saskatchewan Museum search for fossils in the T-rex quarry near Eastend.*

and camping. Unlike Grasslands National Park, where no services exist, Prince Albert includes the small village of Waskesiu within its borders. Waskesiu is situated on a lake and offers tourist amenities such as hotels, shops, restaurants, and even a golf course.

Saskatchewan's lively cultural scene, its diverse museums and galleries, and its exciting variety of outdoor attractions and parks provide the people of the province an abundance of opportunities to enrich body and soul. Yet Saskatchewan has its troubles too, ranging from its rapidly aging farming population to high crime rates in Regina and Saskatoon. Factors such as the province's geographic isolation and its difficulties in developing a diverse economy mean that it will continue to face challenging issues in the near future.

Current Challenges

S askatchewan promotes its attractiveness as a place to live and work by boasting that it has long devoted considerable attention to health care and education. It offers diverse recreational opportunities. The cost of living, especially for housing and land prices, is low in Saskatchewan's cities compared to American, Japanese, and European cities. The province is centrally located in North America and Canada and has reliable energy sources and utilities. These advantages have been recognized in a number of economic and lifestyle surveys. Most recently, an international study conducted in 2002 by the consulting firm KPMG that rated 115 cities according to their overall cost of doing business gave high rankings to Saskatchewan's cities, with Prince Albert placing thirteenth overall and Moose Jaw fifteenth.

A number of storm clouds on the horizon, however, threaten to cast a pall over this rosy picture. Saskatchewan faces serious challenges not only on the economic front but socially and politically. Farmers are giving up as their children move to cities and as natural disasters, from drought to swarms of grasshoppers, make profitable farming impossible. The provincial economy is still somewhat dependent on commodities, such as wheat and oil, whose volatile, internationally set prices cause boom-and-bust business cycles. Saskatchewan's brain drain—its loss of young professionals to Alberta and elsewhere—and its ongoing population decline hinder economic growth. Social services such as health care and education, already showing signs of fraying under budgetary pressures, may face an even tougher time as the province's relatively well-off white population becomes older while at the same time the relatively poor native population becomes younger—and quite likely much larger. Signs of social stress, such as Saskatchewan's high rate of crime, are already evident. The province's reputation for cooperative action and progressive social solutions will face serious challenges from such issues in the near future.

The Disappearing Family Farm

Saskatchewan's reputation as a province of salt-of-the-earth family farmers is in danger of withering away as farms become fewer, larger, and more mechanized every year. The number of farms in the province fell from roughly fifty-seven thousand to fifty thousand alone in the five-year period from 1996 to 2001. Because the total number of acres being cultivated has remained more or less constant, it is clear that the average size of farms is increasing. Whereas the average farm was 400 acres (162 hectares) in 1936, it was 1,152 acres (466 hectares) in 1996 and 1,282 acres (519 hectares) in 2001.

It is Saskatchewan's small farms in particular that are going out of business or being absorbed into larger farms. From 1995 to 2000, those farms reporting gross receipts of at least $500,000 grew in number by 187 percent, while those with gross receipts of less than $10,000 fell from nine thousand to six thousand farms. Roughly half of Saskatchewan's farms are medium-sized, earning $50,000 to $250,000 per year. The profits that these sales earn are so slim, however, that one recent estimate was that the average annual income for Saskatchewan farmers (whose average age is now approaching sixty) in 1999 was less than $2,000!

Not surprisingly, the sons and daughters of these farmers are increasingly reluctant to follow in their parents' steps as they retire. Census figures confirm that Saskatchewan's residents have increasingly been leaving farms and rural towns for the cities. Saskatchewan's rural population has shrunk from 57 percent of the total population in 1961 to 37 percent today. Farm towns like Mendham, near the Alberta border due west of Regina, were tiny in 1961, with 231 people, but are on the verge of disappearing into ghost towns today: Mendham's current population is 40.

In the summer of 2002 the problems many farmers faced almost seemed to reach biblical proportions. More than a dozen Saskatchewan towns experienced record low tempera-

tures for August when a frost swept across the province on the first day of the month, potentially harming crops as far south as Estevan. In addition to the record early frosts, parts of the province also suffered from one of the worst grasshopper infestations in a decade. "This is the year of plague," University of Saskatchewan agronomy professor Steve Shirtliffe lamented to the *Saskatoon StarPhoenix*. "Drought and heat and locusts and frost. What more are we going to get?"[26] It is the first of these plagues—drought—that seems now to be threatening the very existence of agriculture in Saskatchewan.

■ *Saskatchewan photographer Brent Hume took this photo of Wes Doty as part of the series* Neighbours, *which documents the spirit of southeastern Saskatchewan's farming community.*

Return of the Dirty Thirties?

The prairie-wide drought of 1988–1989 was the worst in Canada since the Dirty Thirties, costing the federal government more than $1 billion in crop insurance payments and leading to widespread farm abandonment. The more recent dry spell, ongoing since 1996, threatens to become even more disastrous for Saskatchewan. This drought is not prairie-wide but rather concentrated in parts of the northern prairies and the parkland belt, from the area of Lloydminster to Saskatoon and Prince Albert. (The corresponding patch of land west into Alberta is suffering from the same drought conditions.) Annual precipitation on average was 40 to 60 percent below normal for much of this area in recent years. Saskatoon and Kindersley experienced their driest years on record in 2001.

Persistent drought conditions are devastating for farmers, ranchers, and wildlife. The availability of water, whether from rainfall or irrigation, is the most important factor in determining how much of a crop can be harvested in a semiarid climate like southern Saskatchewan's. In other words, add an inch of rain to an acre of wheat and the result will be a harvest that is larger on average by three or four bushels. Of course, below a certain level of watering, no crop at all will be able to grow. Ranchers face a similar restriction: Pasture lands that are too dry will not supply the forage necessary to support a herd of cattle. Small marshes that dry up limit the breeding area for ducks and other waterfowl, and larger animals like pronghorn antelope suffer from lack of suitable grassland forage.

During the summer of 2002 the drought was so severe in parts of Saskatchewan and Alberta that some cattle farmers

■ *A pair of pronghorn antelope stand in the tall grasses of southern Saskatchewan.*

■ The Prairie Drought Project's Bad News

Even if drought insurance and similar government programs are successful, the frequency and severity of prairie droughts is a cause for concern about the long-term viability of prairie farming. The Prairie Drought Project, a major study conducted by Peter Leavitt and colleagues at the University of Regina and Queen's University in Kingston, Ontario, recently came to sobering conclusions about the likelihood of future drought conditions in the province. The researchers took core samples from sediments underlying six lakes in the prairie provinces. They analyzed the samples for factors relating to salinity and the presence of certain algal fossils. This allowed the researchers to infer how warm and dry the past weather was. After extensive analysis the researchers compiled a historical drought record for the prairies that goes back two thousand years. They determined that severe droughts on the prairies are common, have a rapid onset, and last an average of five to ten years. Moreover, extreme droughts like the one in the 1930s occur every sixty to one hundred years, and drought frequency is likely to be worsened by global warming. The study also found that the twentieth century was wetter than normal, not drier. It was not an encouraging report for the future of prairie farming.

■ *Prairie Drought Project researchers collect an undisturbed core of lake mud by pushing a tube slowly into the sediments.*

were being forced to sell off their entire herds, since they lacked the water and feed necessary to keep the cattle alive. Many farmers were trying to buy hay from parts of eastern Canada or Montana but transportation costs were high. Without hay to feed the cattle over the winter, herds could not survive.

The latest drought prompted the federal government to commit to investing $190 million in a number of initiatives to make farm operations more sustainable and to help farmers deal with dry cycles. The new programs will include constructing small-scale pipelines to expand the prairie's water supply, planting shelterbelts, promoting the digging of dugouts, and expanding tax deferral and crop insurance programs to benefit farmers and ranchers.

■ Potash Capital of the World

For the past thirty years Saskatchewan's ten potash mines have produced more of this useful mineral product than any single country in the world. Saskatchewan accounts for more than 90 percent of Canada's potash production (New Brunswick has the country's only other potash mine) and supplies almost one-third of the world market. Saskatchewan's potash reserves are so large—40 percent of the world's total—they could meet global demand for the mineral for at least the next century and possibly much longer.

North American Indians were among the first to recognize the value of potash as a fertilizer. Many centuries ago they made a crude form of potash by burning broad-leaved trees and spreading the potassium-rich ashes on crops. Pioneers in the seventeenth century refined the process somewhat by adding water to wood ash and boiling the solution in large iron pots— hence the name potash. This type of tree-derived potash developed into an export industry for the Canadian colonies by the mid–eighteenth century. Canada's "asheries" were made obsolete, however, in the late nineteenth century when German scientists found a more efficient way to derive potash from mineral salts.

Saskatchewan owes its status as the world capital of potash to oil drillers. The drilling of an exploratory oil mine in 1943 in Radville, a small town west of Estevan in southern Saskatchewan, revealed a layer of potash

Beyond Wheat and Oil

Long-term droughts can be devastating to Saskatchewan's economy because agriculture remains a major provider of jobs and income. The Saskatchewan government thus has taken steps in recent years to diversify the overall provincial economy. The ranking of most economically important natural resources for Saskatchewan has shifted radically from the beaver furs and buffalo hides of the nineteenth century to today's lumber, mining, and energy. Much of Saskatchewan's future economic growth is now expected to be tied to such natural resources as potash, oil, natural gas, coal, and uranium.

Though less so than Alberta, Saskatchewan is also at the mercy of internationally determined prices for oil and natural gas. The stagnant energy prices of the late 1990s, and the post–September 11, 2001, recession that trimmed energy demand, caused marked declines in provincial revenue generated by at a depth of more than a mile (two kilometers). This was too deep to mine economically, but it inspired potash exploration. By the early 1960s commercial production of potash was on its way in the province. Today more than three thousand workers are employed in Saskatchewan's $2 billion-per-year potash industry. Most of Saskatchewan's potash is exported by rail to the United States.

Saskatchewan's commercial potash deposits lie at an average depth of approximately three thousand feet (one thousand meters). Potash producers sink shafts to the deposits, which are typically flat beds about ten to twenty feet (three to seven meters) thick. Workers use powerful drilling machines to tunnel through the mineral. The potash is transported to the surface where it is refined in industrial plants into powder or granules.

Farmers apply potash to fields of corn, soybeans, wheat, rice, and other crops to replace the potassium that plants take out of the soil as a nutrient. Potassium plays a key role in root growth, mineral absorption, pest resistance, and overall crop yield.

■ *Various postage stamps have honored Canada's miners.*

the energy industry. The reduced revenue came at a time when the federal government was increasingly asking the nation's cities, provinces, and territories to shoulder the burden of social programs, including health care and education. The leaders of Saskatchewan and other provinces have complained in recent years that Ottawa mandates programs but does not provide the cash, or allow provinces the necessary tax freedom, to pay for the programs.

New Economic Directions

The debate over the economic future of the province has engaged politicians, business leaders, environmentalists, and workers. Their views often conflict. For example, proponents of quick growth have proposed sharp increases in the extraction and sale of the province's natural resources. This might include dramatically increasing logging of the provincial forests, as the provincial government proposed in 1999. It also

■ *Oil derricks are an increasingly common sight amidst Saskatchewan's wheat fields.*

might include digging more coal mines, drilling for more oil, and constructing more pipelines to transport oil or natural gas. One political leader recently suggested building a nuclear reactor in Saskatchewan to export power to the United States.

Environmentalists and many others in Saskatchewan view such quick-growth approaches as shortsighted. They point out that the planned doubling of the provincial forestry industry would have the unwanted effects of limiting recreational opportunities, reducing wildlife habitat, and lowering air and water quality. Environmentalists say that logging and mining developments need to be balanced with protected areas that can provide traditional sustainable uses such as fishing, hunting, trapping, and camping. They note that the province's forested regions may already have as many people working in the tourist industry as the forestry industry. Ecotourism in particular is a growing sector of the economy in Saskatchewan and elsewhere as people look for more meaningful ways to spend vacation time.

Historically, Saskatchewan has not been as active as some provinces in protecting wilderness areas. In recent years, however, it has taken steps to substantially increase the amount of protected land by establishing new provincial parks and reserves. Since 1992 Saskatchewan's total protected acreage, including the two national parks, has approximately doubled, to 6 percent of the land (which is still half the figure for British Columbia). Environmentalists contend that some of the province's unique ecological areas remain underrepresented, including native grasslands and wilderness in the heavily logged southern edge of the boreal forest, such as in the vicinity of Doré Lake northwest of Prince Albert National Park.

■ The Promise of Ecotourism

Surveys suggest that more and more people in Saskatchewan are taking part in the type of nature-based recreational activities that support ecotourism. The activities that are growing the fastest include birdwatching, hiking, and backpacking, all of which increased by more than 70 percent from 1983 to 1995 according to one survey. Other outdoor recreational activities increasing in popularity include photography, diving, learning about nature and different cultures, fishing, and foraging for nontimber forest products such as mushrooms, berries, and medicinal plants. Saskatchewan offers a number of advantages as a site for such ecotourist activities, including "the diversity of its natural resources; strength in waterfowl and shorebird populations; the lack of crowding and pollution; the existing networks of protected areas, vacation farms, and lodges; and a rich complementary cultural heritage with a strong First Nations component," economist David Bruce Weaver noted in *Canadian Geographer.*

Proponents of ecotourism say that it offers a viable complementary industry, with jobs that range from backcountry guides to researchers, for northern communities that are otherwise totally dependent upon forestry to fuel the local economy. The Ecotourism Society of Saskatchewan, formed in 1998, supports the principle of using some of the funds derived from ecotourism to help maintain the local resource base and the culture of the local people. Currently, eight Saskatchewan ecotourism operators have been approved for tours and/or accommodations and six provincial parks have been certified as ecotourist destinations.

■ *Saskatchewan's many lakes and rivers attract enthusiastic kayakers and canoeists.*

Stemming the "Brain Drain"

An educated workforce is crucial for running today's diversified economy, and Saskatchewan in recent years has experienced a disappointing inability to hang on to its best and brightest young professionals. A 1999 Royal Bank of Canada study determined that Saskatchewan's overall net outflow to other provinces was 2.3 percent from 1991 to 1996 but that this figure represented more than 8 percent of the province's university graduates. One estimate is that more than half a million Saskatchewan-born residents have moved out of the province in the past fifty years. This "brain drain" is reflected in the shrinking total population, the increasing average age of provincial residents, and low immigration rates.

Surprisingly, Saskatchewan's total population today is barely up from the early 1930s, when it reached more than 920,000, and it has been falling pretty steadily for almost two decades since hitting a peak of about 1 million in 1986. During the most recent census period, from 1996 to 2001, its growth was negative (-1.1 percent). At the same time the population, as in much of the rest of Canada, is aging. Fully 15 percent of Saskatchewan's population is now age sixty-five or greater. Moreover, in recent times the province has been averaging merely two thousand new immigrants per year, a tiny fraction of the quarter-million that Canada attracts. A large majority of the country's immigrants prefer the diverse economic opportunities available in Ontario and, to a lesser extent, the western provinces of Alberta and British Columbia. Today only 5 percent of Saskatchewan's population is foreign-born.

Alberta and British Columbia also seem to be the principal destinations for those who leave Saskatchewan. Saskatchewan residents who move there often cite the lure of lower taxes, more jobs, and higher salaries. "If people are Saskatchewan's greatest export, Alberta is the biggest beneficiary," said writer Michelle Harries in *Maclean's*. "This is particularly true in Calgary, where even a former mayor hails from the province next door." Harries went on to note, "So many have answered that siren call there's even a thriving Saskatchewan Social Club in Calgary."[27]

An Increasingly Native Population

Natives are the one group that seems committed to staying in Saskatchewan. The province is already neck-and-neck with

Manitoba in terms of having the highest percentage of aboriginal residents among Canadian provinces. (Nunavut and the Northwest Territories have majority indigenous populations.) Unlike the aging general population, Saskatchewan's aboriginal population is relatively young and exhibits a high birth rate. Over the past twenty years the Saskatchewan aboriginal population has more than doubled. The current population of approximately 140,000 aboriginals (70 percent First Nations and the rest Métis), up from 110,000 in 1996, is expected to grow in leaps and bounds over the next decade. If the current native growth rate remains at about 5 percent annually, demographers say that the native population will reach 200,000 by 2010. A more conservative estimate assumes a slower growth rate but that by 2045 the aboriginal population will nevertheless represent one-third of the province's total.

The rapidly growing native population has been slow to benefit from social and economic reforms. Aboriginal people suffer from a rate of tuberculosis that is fifteen times the provincial norm and a diabetes rate that is three times as high. In 1996–1997 a shocking 74 percent of the provincial prison admissions were aboriginals. Native people today earn an average annual income that is barely more than half the nonnative rate. One in five natives living on reserves do not have access to safe drinking water. Only half of the houses on reserves are considered to provide adequate living conditions for residents. About half of all aboriginal children living in Regina and Saskatoon are being raised by a single parent, usually the mother. It almost goes without saying that natives in Saskatchewan suffer from much higher than provincial average rates of poverty, unemployment, suicide, and a host of other social indicators.

These long-standing problems have proved to be difficult to solve. Both the provincial and the federal governments have been more willing during the past decade to make land grants to native tribes and to fund social programs that target native health problems, unemployment, education, and business development. The challenge for the provincial government is to continue meaningful funding during times of budgetary scarcity. Another challenge is to avoid the tendency of some government funding to create the stratified societies found in some tribes, wherein an often-male-dominated clique of power brokers makes decisions that enrich themselves and a few others but leave the vast majority of the tribe as poor as ever.

The overall poverty of Saskatchewan's relatively large native population is reflected in the below-average rankings the province earns in a number of important health indicators, including infant mortality rate. In a 1996 ranking of the provinces and territories Saskatchewan finished next-to-last, with an infant mortality rate that was almost double that of Quebec, the top-ranked province. Saskatchewan has a relatively high percentage of smokers and it recently tied with Newfoundland for the worst rate of heavy drinking among the provinces. Perhaps most surprisingly, Saskatchewan today suffers from higher rates of crime than in any other province.

A Stubborn Crime Problem

In 2001 Saskatchewan had the worst provincial crime rate in the country for the fourth consecutive year (the territories typically have even higher rates). Its overall crime rate of more than thirteen thousand offenses per one hundred thousand residents was almost double the national average.

■ The Mean Streets of Regina and Saskatoon

Saskatchewan's two principal cities are particularly crime plagued. Both Regina and Saskatoon average about a half dozen murders per year. This may be low by U.S. standards—the similarly sized city of Richmond, Virginia, averaged about one hundred murders per year from 1996 to 2001—but it is high by Canadian standards. In fact, Regina and Saskatoon have the highest and second-highest homicide rates among the twenty-five metropolitan areas of Canada. The homicide rate of 3.5 per 100,000 residents in Regina is seven times as high as the rate in London, Ontario, a city twice Regina's size. Regina and Saskatoon also have the unfortunate distinction of being number one and two among metro areas for rates of violent crime and overall crime. Regina's property crime rate is 286 percent higher than Toronto's. Regina is the car-theft capital of Canada, a fact that was highlighted in February 2002 when the provincial justice minister, Chris Axwothy, had his Chrysler stolen in Regina immediately prior to a news conference he had scheduled on government plans to crack down on car thieves.

Saskatchewan has Canada's highest violent crime rate and second-highest murder rate. It also has among the worst figures in Canada for drinking and driving, property crime (which dropped in every province in 2000 except for Saskatchewan), and teen suicide.

The reasons for this ongoing crime wave have been much debated in Saskatchewan. Among the most commonly cited factors are the inability of the province to raise the average income rate among the working class, the gap between the rich and the poor in Saskatchewan, and the province's relatively low average education levels. Another possible factor is that Saskatchewan's cities, unlike the rest of the province, on average are becoming younger. The 2001 census showed that the Saskatoon metro area now has the youngest population in the country, with a median age of 34.3 years compared to 36.7 for Saskatchewan as a whole. Regina was also in the top ten for youth. Youths, particularly those in the sixteen- to twenty-four-year-old age group, are more likely to commit crimes than younger or older people.

"While we have been doing a lot, we simply have not addressed effectively this crime rate problem," said provincial justice minister Chris Axworthy. "We haven't effectively addressed the social marginalization problem and the numbers of young people who face significant social challenges. Only if we solve that problem can we address the overall crime rate problem."[28] He noted that the areas with the worst crime are the inner cities and the aboriginal communities. Government and police initiatives to curb crime include everything from aboriginal worker programs to night basketball leagues.

Toward a Reinvigorated Saskatchewan Identity

During the last few years aboriginal culture has been reinvigorated by a renewed emphasis on traditional practices, ceremonies, and languages. Likewise, the province as a whole is looking for ways to overcome the problems and practices—such as the extraction of western resources for the benefit of the manufacturing and financial sectors of the east—that have prevented it from building on the success and promise it showed during its first decade as a province.

As Saskatchewan approaches its centennial year in 2005, its people are struggling with important questions that will

■ *Buffalo ranching has become an important industry in Saskatchewan.*

largely determine the province's future over the next century. How can it cope with a diminishing rural and farming heritage, as evidenced by the abandonment of family farms, the shutting of rural schools, and the declining rural population? Are the many small towns in the province doomed to continue to lose their young people, whether to Saskatchewan's cities or urban places elsewhere? Will rural Saskatchewan turn into a civic graveyard of ghost towns, fading away as they lose a critical mass of residents—and the tax base—needed to survive?

By the same token, how will Saskatchewan manage its extensive resources? The province no longer has a one-dimensional, wheat-dependent economy. But is Saskatchewan in danger of falling into a similar trap by relying too exclusively on energy or mineral resources that are, ultimately, finite? Perhaps not. In 2002, with major funding from the federal government, Saskatchewan opened its first commercial wind power project in the Gull Lake area west of Swift Current. The provincial government is also hoping to reap the rewards from investing not only in forestry and mining but fringe industries ranging from ethanol (a grain-based fuel) production to designer livestock (like buffalo and llamas) ranching.

Saskatchewan has its rich history of cooperative action to sustain its quest for future success. More than a thousand co-ops, covering retailing, distribution, and service functions, remain active in the province today, with one in every two Saskatchewan residents maintaining a membership in one or more. It is this tradition of social concern that may ultimately be the deciding factor in Saskatchewan, a province that is, observed *National Post* columnist Roy MacGregor recently, "the most Canadian of provinces, the centre, the core, the land where the most significant trait of Canadian history as well as its literature—survival—is still a tenuous, day-to-day prospect."[29]

Facts About Saskatchewan

Government

- Form: Parliamentary system with federal and provincial levels
- Highest official: Premier, who administers provincial legislation and regulations
- Capital: Regina
- Entered confederation: September 1, 1905 (same date as Alberta, making the two the eighth and ninth provinces)
- Provincial flag: Green band represents Saskatchewan's northern forests, gold band symbolizes the southern grain areas, with the provincial shield of arms and the floral emblem, the western red lily
- Motto: "From many peoples, strength"

Land

- Area: 251,866 square miles (652,333 square kilometers); 6.5% of total land of Canada; fifth-largest province; rivers and lakes cover 12.5% of Saskatchewan's territory
- Boundaries: Bounded on the north by the Northwest Territories, on the west by Alberta, on the south by Montana and North Dakota, and on the east by Manitoba
- National parks: Grasslands, Prince Albert

- Provincial parks: thirty-five, plus some 250 recreation sites and regional parks, encompassing approximately 15,000 square miles (39,000 square kilometers); the largest provincial park is Lac La Ronge in central Saskatchewan
- Highest point: 4,567 feet (1,392 meters), unnamed peak in the Cypress Hills
- Largest lake: Athabasca (partly in Alberta), 3,058 square miles (7,920 square kilometers); fourth-largest lake entirely within Canada and twenty-first-largest lake in world
- Other major lakes: Reindeer (fifth-largest lake entirely within Canada), Wollaston, La Ronge, Cree, Peter Pond, Diefenbaker
- Longest river: Saskatchewan (North and South), 1,205 miles (1,939 kilometers); fourth-longest in Canada
- Other major rivers: Qu'Appelle, Churchill, Battle
- Time zones: Mountain Standard Time (Lloydminster) and Central Standard Time
- Geographical extremes: 49° N to 60° N latitude; 101° W to 110° W longitude

Climate

- Longest windchill event: 215 hours, December 1978 in Saskatoon (Canadian record)
- Most sunshine: 2,540 hours per year, Estevan (Canadian record)
- Highest temperature: 113°F (45°C) at Midale and Yellow Grass, on July 5, 1937 (Canadian record)
- Lowest temperature: −70°F (−57°C) at Prince Albert, 1893

People

- Population: 978,933 (2001 census); sixth-highest population of provinces and territories; 3.3% of Canada's total population of 30,007,094
- Annual growth rate: −1.1% from 1996 to 2001 (fifth-slowest growth rate among provinces and territories)
- Density: 3.9 persons per square mile, compared to Canadian national average of 7.8 (1.5 and 3.0 persons per square kilometer)
- Location: 63% urban; 37% rural; 23% of residents live in the Saskatoon metropolitan area

- Predominant heritages: British, aboriginal
- Largest ethnic groups: German, Austrian, Ukrainian, French
- Major religious groups: Catholic, Protestant, Mennonite, Greek Orthodox
- Primary languages (first learned and still understood): 84% English, 2% French, and 14% other languages, led by German and aboriginal
- Largest metropolitan areas: Saskatoon, population 225,927, an increase of 3.1% between 1996 and 2001; seventeenth-largest metropolitan area in Canada; Regina, 192,800, −0.4%, eighteenth-largest
- Other major cities: Prince Albert, Moose Jaw, Lloydminster (partly in Alberta), Yorkton, North Battleford
- Life expectancy at birth, 3-year average 1995–1997: Men 75.4 years; women 81.4; total both sexes 78.3; fourth among provinces and territories (Canadian average: Men 75.4; women 81.2; total 78.4)
- Immigration 7/1/2000–6/30/2001: 1,845, 0.7% of Canadian total of 252,088; sixth-highest of provinces and territories
- Births 7/1/2000–6/30/2001: 12,541
- Deaths 7/1/2000–6/30/2001: 9,266
- Marriages in 1998: 5,730
- Divorces in 1998: 2,246

Plants and Animals

- Provincial animal: White-tailed deer
- Provincial bird: Sharp-tailed grouse
- Provincial flower: Western red lily
- Provincial tree: White birch
- Provincial grass: Needle-and-thread grass
- Endangered, threatened, or vulnerable species: ten, including burrowing owl, piping plover, whooping crane, swift fox, hairy prairie clover, and sand verbena

Holidays

- National: January 1 (New Year's Day); Good Friday; Easter; Easter Monday; Monday preceding May 25 (Victoria or Dollard Day); July 1 or, if this date falls on a

Sunday, July 2 (Canada's birthday); 1st Monday of September (Labour Day); 2nd Monday of October (Thanksgiving); November 11 (Remembrance Day); December 25 (Christmas); December 26 (Boxing Day)

- Provincial: 1st Monday in August (Saskatchewan Day)

Economy

- Gross domestic product per capita: $26,094 in 1999, sixth among provinces and territories and 77.1% compared to U.S. average[30]

- Gross provincial product: $31.4 billion at market prices in 2000, sixth among the provinces and territories and 3.1% of gross national product

- Major exports: wheat and other grains, petroleum, potash, uranium, natural gas

- Agriculture: wheat (produces 54% of nation's supply), canola, rye, oats, barley, cattle, hogs, poultry

- Tourism: hiking, sightseeing, golfing, fishing, hunting, canoeing

- Logging: softwood lumber, particle board and plywood, posts and poles

- Manufacturing: food products, agricultural implements and chemicals, transportation equipment, machinery

- Mining: potash (world's largest producer), uranium (world's largest producer), crude oil (Canada's second-largest producer), coal (Canada's third-largest producer), natural gas, copper, zinc, salt, sand and gravel, gold, peat, clay

Notes

Introduction: The Heartland of Canada

1. Quoted in "Happy Trails to Roy," *CBC Radio*, September 28, 2000. http://radio.cbc.ca.
2. Peter Gzowski, "In Search of Canada's Heartland," *Maclean's*, February 4, 2002.

Chapter 1: Land of Living Skies

3. Quoted in "Cypress Hills," Canadian Snapshots, *Canadian Geographic*. www.canadiangeographic.ca.
4. *Government of Saskatchewan*, Government Relations and Aboriginal Affairs, "About Saskatchewan: Climate." www.immigrationsask.gov.sk.ca.

Chapter 2: The Lure of Beaver and Buffalo

5. David Meyer, "Human History in Far Northern Saskatchewan," *Canoe Saskatchewan*. www.lights.com.
6. *Indian and Northern Affairs Canada*, First Nations in Canada, "The Culture Areas: A Survey." www.ainc-inac.gc.ca.
7. Quoted in "Prelude to Western Agriculture," *Agriculture and Agri-Food Canada*. www.agr.gc.ca.
8. *University of Calgary*, Applied History Research Group, Calgary and Southern Alberta, "John Palliser, Henry Youle Hind and Simon Dawson." www.ucalgary.ca.
9. *"Reports of Progress . . . on the Assiniboine and Saskatchewan Exploring Expedition,* 1859, by Henry Youle Hind," *National Archives of Canada.* www.archives.ca.

10. *National Archives of Canada*, The Canadian West, "Expedition of the North-West Mounted Police of Canada into the Saskatchewan Territory." www.archives.ca.

11. *Legislative Assembly of Alberta*, Office of the Lieutenant-Governor, Assembly Support Services, Library Services, Publications, "Seats of Government (Capitals)." www.assembly.ab.ca.

Chapter 3: A Cooperative Tradition

12. *Citizenship and Immigration Canada,* Forging Our Legacy: Canadian Citizenship and Immigration 1900–1977, "The Arrival of the Europeans." www.cic.gc.ca.

13. *National Archives of Canada*, The Canadian West, "Saskatoon, Sask.: The City of Unlimited Possibilities." www.archives.ca.

14. Stephan Symko, "Discovery of Marquis Wheat," Research Centres: Business, Research and Innovation, *Agriculture and Agri-Food Canada.* http://res2.agr.ca.

15. Quoted in Gura Bharvava, "A City Divided by Political Philosophies: Residential Development in a Bi-Provincial City in Canada," *American Journal of Economics and Sociology*, January 2001, pp. 317–73.

16. David Laycock, "The Prairie Roots of Canada's Political 'Third Parties,'" Western Canadian Development and Political Protest, 1867–1914, The Centre for Canadian Studies, *Mount Allison University*. www.mta.ca.

17. *Yzowl's Truly Canadian Links and Information*, Saskatchewan, "History of the Province." http://trulycanadian.freeservers.com.

18. W.E. Garrett, "Canada's Heartland, the Prairie Provinces," *National Geographic*, October 1970, p. 476.

19. Marlene Piturro, Ph.D., "Some Lessons to Be Learned from Canadian Health System," *Managed Care*, March 2002. www.managedcaremag.com.

20. *Pundit Magazine*, "Rising Stars and Sinking Ships," April 8, 2001. www.punditmag.com.

Chapter 4: Daily Life

21. Jay and Audrey Walz, *Portrait of Canada*. New York: American Heritage Press, 1970, p. 278.

22. George E. Hickie, "Dwindling Returns for Farmers," *Regina Leader-Post*, August 29, 2002. www.canada.com.

23. Quoted in Paul Yanko, "Living Off the Land," *Virtual Saskatchewan*. www.virtualsk.com.

Chapter 5: Arts and Culture

24. Mark Lightbody, Thomas Huhti, and Ryan Ver Berkmoes, *Canada*. Hawthorn, Australia: Lonely Planet, 1999, p. 685.

25. Dennis Bueckert, "Moose Jaw Tunnels Reveal Dark Tales of Canada's Past," *Canadian Press*. www.canoe.ca.

Chapter 6: Current Challenges

26. Quoted in Michelle Lang, "August Chill Smashes Records," *Saskatoon StarPhoenix*, August 3, 2002. www.canada.com.

27. Michelle Harries, "The Road to Success Often Leads to Alberta," *Maclean's*, July 15, 2002. www.macleans.com.

28. Quoted in James Parker, "Saskatchewan Leads Nation in Crime," *Saskatoon StarPhoenix*, July 18, 2002. www.canada.com.

29. Roy MacGregor, "Premier Resists Siren Song of Tax Cuts," *National Post*, August 20, 1999. www.nationalpost.com.

Facts About Saskatchewan

30. *Demographia*, "Canada: Regional Gross Domestic Product Data: 1999." www.demographia.com.

Chronology

B.C.

ca. 11,000   The earliest native people enter the area from the west.

ca. 5000   Woodland hunter-gatherers live in the forested regions of present-day Saskatchewan.

A.D.

1670   King Charles II of England grants the Hudson's Bay Company a monopoly on the fur trade in all land drained by the Hudson Bay, including much of present-day Saskatchewan.

1690   Henry Kelsey begins his two-year journey from the Hudson Bay to the prairies of southern present-day Saskatchewan.

1730s   French Canadian explorer La Vérendrye and sons explore parts of the Saskatchewan River and build fur-trading posts.

1750s   Plains Cree obtain horses.

1774   Samuel Hearne of the Hudson's Bay Company establishes a fur-trading post at Cumberland House on Cumberland Lake, which becomes the oldest continuously occupied site in Saskatchewan.

1796   British-born explorer and mapmaker David Thompson is the first European to explore north of the Churchill River to Lake Athabasca.

1821   Hudson's Bay and North West companies merge.

1857   John Palliser initiates a three-year exploration of the prairies that sets the stage for future settlement and transportation patterns.

1867   Ontario, Quebec, Nova Scotia, and New Brunswick form the Dominion of Canada.

1870   Canada purchases Rupert's Land from the Hudson's Bay Company and establishes the North-West Territories.

1872   Dominion Lands Act offers free homesteads to settlers.

1882   Canada establishes the District of Saskatchewan, named after the river, in the North-West Territories, with Regina as capital; Canadian Pacific Railway reaches Regina on its way to becoming, three years later, Canada's first transcontinental railway.

1883   A few dozen members of an Ontario temperance society found Saskatoon on the banks of the South Saskatchewan River.

1885   The Northwest Rebellion is crushed by the federal government.

1887   Canada establishes North America's first federal bird sanctuary at Last Mountain Lake, between Regina and Saskatoon.

1896–1910   The federal government funds an ambitious campaign to attract Canadian and European settlers to the prairies.

1905   On September 1 Saskatchewan and Alberta are carved out of the North-West Territories to become Canada's eighth and ninth provinces.

1911   Expanding wheat sales and steady immigration turn prosperous Saskatchewan into Canada's third-largest province.

1916   Women gain the right to vote in provincial elections, two years before Canada grants all women suffrage.

1919   Saskatchewan School Act makes English only legal language of instruction, in effect banning English-French and English-Ukrainian bilingual schools.

1930   Canadian government transfers control over Saskatchewan's natural resources to the provincial government.

1930s   The Great Depression, the Dust Bowl drought, and falling wheat prices lead to widespread poverty and turmoil in Saskatchewan.

1932   Progressive laborers and farmers from the prairie provinces form the Co-operative Commonwealth Federation (CCF), a democratic socialist party.

1933   At its meeting in Regina, the CCF adopts the Regina Manifesto, calling for nationalization of key industries and establishment of progressive social programs including health and unemployment insurance.

1944   Under Thomas C. Douglas the CCF wins the provincial election, making Saskatchewan the site of the first socialist government in North America.

1953   The province's first significant oilfield is discovered in Midale in southeast Saskatchewan.

1957   Saskatchewan lawyer and politician John Diefenbaker elected as Canada's thirteenth prime minister.

1961–1962   The provincial government introduces Canada's first publicly funded health care program for the poor.

1962   Large-scale potash production begins.

1974   Provincial 1919 School Act is revised to allow bilingual instruction.

1991   Roy Romanow of the New Democratic Party (NDP) is elected provincial premier, the first one in Canada of Ukrainian heritage.

1997   After a dozen former government officials face corruption charges, the PCP disbands; a coalition of conservatives and liberals forms the Saskatchewan Party (SP), which becomes the official opposition to the ruling NDP.

1999   The rural-based SP makes a strong showing in legislative elections, though the NDP retains control of the government.

2001   New NDP leader Lorne Calvert replaces Romanow as premier; Romanow agrees to head a federal commission to reform health care.

For Further Reading

Books

Robert Bothwell, *A Traveller's History of Canada*. New York: Interlink Books, 2002. An up-to-date summary of major events, with useful maps.

Meika Lalonde, Elton Laclare, and Ralph Nilson, eds., *Discover Saskatchewan: A Guide to Historic Sites*. Regina: Canadian Plains Research Center, 1998. Details not only sites but also museums; maps included.

Mark Lightbody, Thomas Huhti, and Ryan Ver Berkmoes, *Canada*. Hawthorn, Australia: Lonely Planet, 1999. An informative and practical guide to the country's features, with a good section on Saskatchewan.

Reader's Digest, *Canada Coast to Coast*. Montreal: Reader's Digest Association (Canada), 1998. Offers brief descriptions of towns and things to see along Canada's principal highways.

Websites

Government of Saskatchewan (www.gov.sk.ca). The provincial website offers numerous links to background information on legislation, ministries, attractions, and the like.

Saskatchewan Interactive (http://interactive.usask.ca). A fun and useful source for facts and figures on the province's agriculture, forestry, mining, tourism, and more.

Virtual Saskatchewan (www.virtualsk.com). This online magazine offers an abundance of well-written articles about provincial sites and attractions.

Works Consulted

Books

Wayne Curtis et al., *Frommer's Canada*. New York: Simon and Schuster, 1998. This is an excellent travel guide to the country.

Irene Spry, ed., *The Papers of the Palliser Expedition, 1857–1860*. Toronto: Champlain Society, 1968. A collection of primary documents.

Wallace Stegner, *Wolf Willow: A History, a Story, and a Memory of the Last Plains Frontier*. New York: Viking, 1962. The noted writer offers anecdotes as well as history lessons relating to the site of his boyhood home in southwestern Saskatchewan.

Wayne C. Thompson, *Canada 2000*. Harpers Ferry, WV: Stryker-Post, 2000. An annually updated look at Canadian culture, history, and politics.

Jay and Audrey Walz, *Portrait of Canada*. New York: American Heritage Press, 1970. A pair of journalists provide an insightful look at the country's history, geography, and people.

Periodicals

Gura Bharvava, "A City Divided by Political Philosophies: Residential Development in a Bi-Provincial City in Canada," *American Journal of Economics and Sociology*, January 2001.

Tom Ford, "Regina—Doing More with Less," *The Heritage Network*, May 1999.

W.E. Garrett, "Canada's Heartland, the Prairie Provinces," *National Geographic*, October 1970.

Peter Gzowski, "In Search of Canada's Heartland," *Maclean's*, February 4, 2002.

Michelle Harries, "The Road to Success Often Leads to Alberta," *Maclean's*, July 15, 2002.

Mary Nemeth, "Disappearing Saskatchewan," *Maclean's*, July 15, 2002.

Marlene Piturro, Ph.D., "Some Lessons to Be Learned from Canadian Health System," *Managed Care*, March 2002.

Michael Snider, "Desperate Journey," *Maclean's*, July 1, 2002.

David Bruce Weaver, "A Regional Framework for Planning Ecotourism in Saskatchewan," *Canadian Geographer*, Fall 1997.

Internet Sources

Agriculture and Agri-Food Canada, "Prelude to Western Agriculture." www.agr.gc.ca.

Allen Sapp Gallery, "Story of His Art." www.allensapp.com.

Canadian Geographic, Canadian Snapshots, "Cypress Hills." www.canadiangeographic.ca.

CBC Radio, "Happy Trails to Roy," September 28, 2000. http://radio.cbc.ca.

Citizenship and Immigration Canada, Forging Our Legacy: Canadian Citizenship and Immigration 1900–1977, "The Arrival of the Europeans." www.cic.gc.ca

Demographia, "Canada: Regional Gross Domestic Product Data: 1999." www.demographia.com.

Indian and Northern Affairs Canada, First Nations in Canada, "The Culture Areas: A Survey"; "First Nation Casino Property Receives Urban Reserve Status," January 31, 2002. www.ainc-inac.gc.ca.

David Laycock, "The Prairie Roots of Canada's Political 'Third Parties,'" Western Canadian Development and Political Protest, 1867–1914, The Centre for Canadian Studies, *Mount Allison University*. www.mta.ca.

Legislative Assembly of Alberta, Office of the Lieutenant-Governor, Assembly Support Services, Library Services, Publications, "Seats of Government (Capitals)." www.assembly.ab.ca.

Roy MacGregor, "Premier Resists Siren Song of Tax Cuts," *National Post.* August 20, 1999, www.nationalpost.com.

Craig I.W. Marlatt, "The Right Honourable John Diefenbaker," *CanadaInfo.* www.craigmarlatt.com.

David Meyer, "Human History in Far Northern Saskatchewan," *Canoe Saskatchewan.* www.lights.com.

Pundit Magazine, "Rising Stars and Sinking Ships," April 8, 2001. www.punditmag.com.

Stephan Symko, "Discovery of Marquis Wheat," Research Centres: Business, Research and Innovation, *Agriculture and Agri-Food Canada.* http://res2.agr.ca.

University of Calgary, Applied History Research Group, Calgary and Southern Alberta, "John Palliser, Henry Youle Hind and Simon Dawson." www.ucalgary.ca.

Yzowl's Truly Canadian Links and Information, Saskatchewan, "History of the Province." http://trulycanadian.freeservers.com.

Websites

Canada.com (www.canada.com). A useful site for access to provincial newspapers such as the *Regina Leader-Post* and *Saskatoon StarPhoenix.*

Canada's Digital Collections (http://collections.ic.gc.ca). Showcases more than four hundred websites celebrating Canada's history, geography, science, technology, and culture.

The Canadian Encyclopedia (www.thecanadianencyclopedia.com). This web version of the three-volume printed work is authoritative and easy to use.

National Archives of Canada (www.archives.ca). "The Canadian West" section offers primary documents and background information on the people and cultures who settled the prairies.

Index

Picture Credits

Cover photo: © Robert Holmes/CORBIS
© The Allen Sapp Gallery, The Gonor Collection, 81
© Archives of Ontario, 44
© Craig Aurness/CORBIS, 24
© Bettmann/CORBIS, 62
© Canada Tourism Commission, 11, 12, 20, 22, 33, 34, 66, 70,
    71, 72,
© Canadian Heritage Gallery, 30
© City of Saskatoon, 77
© CORBIS/Royalty-free, 19, 96, 106
© Getty Images, 101
© Glenbow Archives, 39
© Government of Saskatchewan (RSM), 86, 91
© Brent Hume/Saskatchewan Arts Board Permanent
    Collection, 95
© Limnology Laboratory, University of Regina, 97
© National Archives of Canada, 35, 36, 45, 46, 51, 52, 60, 99,
    100
© Lisa J. Pahkala, 89
© Royal Studios/Bill Dubecky, 78
© Saskatchewan Archives Board, 59
© Saskatchewan Recording Industry Association, 83
© Irene Sosulski/City of Saskatoon, 68
© Paul A. Souders/CORBIS, 40
© Graham Tim/CORBIS SYGMA, 85
© Tourism Saskatchewan, 20
© Tourism Saskatoon, 87
© The Tunnels of Moose Jaw, 90
© University of Saskatchewan, 28, 56, 75

About the Author

Mark Mayell is a freelance writer and editor who has au-
thored five nonfiction books as well as numerous magazine
articles. He lives with his wife and two children in Wellesley,
Massachusetts.